JOSEPH CHAMBERLAIN AND THE THEORY OF IMPERIALISM

Joseph Chamberlain and the Theory of Imperialism

By WILLIAM L. STRAUSS

NEW YORK

Howard Fertig

1971

Copyright 1942 by William L. Strauss

HOWARD FERTIG, INC. EDITION 1971
Published by arrangement with the author

Library of Congress Catalog Card Number: 71-80596

PRINTED IN THE UNITED STATES OF AMERICA
BY NOBLE OFFSET PRINTERS, INC.

TO MOTHER AND DAD

ACKNOWLEDGMENTS

The author began this study at the suggestion of Professor Rupert Emerson of Harvard University. He wishes to express his gratitude for the stimulation, encouragement, and help which Professor Emerson gave him during the course of the preparation of this work. Moreover, he wishes to thank Mr. Robert B. Watson and Miss Lorena Drummond for reading the typescript, and his wife for reading the proofs.

WILLIAM L. STRAUSS

INTRODUCTION

As the cycle of nineteenth century imperialism, in which Joseph Chamberlain played so striking a role, lost its ebullience and faltered into a decline, the theorists took up where the practitioners had left off. On the whole the entire imperialist forward surge fell outside the expectations and prophecies of the principal schools of the day. Not until the movement had already reached its peak did it receive very serious theoretical attention. Looking backward it is possible to discover exceedingly interesting philosophical and scientific trends which can be seen as the forerunners in the realm of ideas of the great events which were taking place in the realm of action, but they were very scantily noticed at the time, if they were noticed at all.

In almost all respects the general currents of opinion in the first half of the nineteenth century, which reach down strongly but far less confidently into our own time, were not only hostile to the type of expansion by force and fraud which characterized imperialist activity, but were committed to a method of analysis which tended to exclude the likelihood of its happening. In economic thought the two dominant schools were the classical economists of the Manchester variety and their brothers (for they shared much the same intellectual heritage) of the Marxist persuasion. Both, in their different ways, looked to a future in which there would be a brotherhood of man arising from the new industrial system and the scientific discoveries upon which it was based. Politically the major lines were the spread of constitutionalism, democracy, and the self-determination of nations, which likewise pointed in the direction of peace and goodwill among men. Wars and revolutions for the attainment of these purposes were conceivable and even justifiable, but they were wars which in each instance, it seemed, worked to eradicate abuses and to eliminate the necessity of further convulsions of the same order. On the greatest scale this was the content and the source of the Wilsonian idealism of the period of the first World War. But, on the other hand, wars which looked to domination and oppression were the outmoded barbarisms of less advanced people, remote from the blessings of modern industrial civilization.

What went wrong with this coherent and highly intelligent body of doctrine? What basic elements were so grossly out of alignment in its method of analysis as to have the world turn in directions almost diametrically opposed to those which were forecast? The answers to these questions remain obscure despite a number of efforts to work them out. The answer which had gained the widest currency, at least until the last decade or so, was that put forward by the Marxists who were forced to cut it almost from the whole cloth and add it to the body of doctrine left by Marx and Engels. The Marxist version, familiar in its outlines if not in its details, lays the entire imperialist process at the doors of capitalism in the last throes preceding its collapse and finds it to be virtually exclusively an economic matter. This belief that the forces generated by capitalism inevitably turn into imperialism found a somewhat naive acceptance in many circles which repudiated the rest of Marxism with indignation.

The most striking shortcoming in the exposition of the Marxist theory of imperialism was that it rested so very largely on purely abstract reasoning. It puts the matter overcrudely but it might be said that the fundamental argument is this: capitalism in its later stages operates in such a way as to require expansion as is shown by analysis of the nature of the capitalist system; imperialist expansion took place at a certain historical period in which capitalism flourished; therefore imperialism is the product and necessary result of capitalism. In recent years a number of studies have been made either of particular imperialist episodes or of outstanding imperialist leaders, and the general tenor of their conclusions has been such as to cast considerable doubt on the exclusive validity of the Marxist thesis. In this book William Strauss carries a stage further the process of undertaking the type of study which is essential if we are gradually to work out a more satisfactory theory of imperialism which will embrace not only abstract analysis but historical facts as well. Joseph Chamberlain is a key figure in the development of British imperialism and Mr. Strauss has presented a challenging interpretation of his career.

RUPERT EMERSON

CONTENTS

The March of Imperialism

Modern imperialism may be said to date from the search for a new route to the East and the resultant discovery of America. In the three centuries following, the European states expanded their control over most of the New World, India, Malaysia, and certain sections of the coast line of Africa which were used as way-stations to India and the East.

In the first three-quarters of the nineteenth century imperialistic expansion was at a low ebb, if not completely dormant. In England this was in part due to the Industrial Revolution and the doctrines expounded by Adam Smith and David Ricardo. The growing popularity of the idea of *laissez faire* and the rise of free trade resulted in the belief that the welfare of humanity could best be served by pursuing a policy of non-intervention in the affairs of others. This led to opposition to the expansion of control over native races. It also gave rise to a campaign to decentralize the control over the British colonies peopled mainly by immigrants from England and to the granting of responsible government to these colonies. There was widespread acceptance of the notion that these colonies would sooner or later become independent; it was believed that separation of the colonies from the mother country was desirable and would be profitable.

Beginning, however, with 1872—the year of Disraeli's significant Crystal Palace Speech—the mood changed. Disraeli ushered in an era of imperialism. Joseph Chamberlain, following Disraeli, became the leader of what was then called the "New Imperialism." This age of British imperialism came to an end with the election of the Liberals in 1906. Roughly within the same period, France, Russia, and Germany engaged in a similar policy of expansion. The rivalries brought on by the imperialistic policies of these states were largely responsible for World War I.

Despite the many obvious defects of the Treaty of Versailles which concluded the "war to end war," many thought that it marked the dawn of a new day. Differences that separated the interests of

1

rival states would be settled by peaceful negotiations; backward peoples would no longer be exploited but would be governed in their own interests for the total good of humanity. It was hoped that commercial relations between nations would be placed on a new footing and that markets and raw materials would be accessible to all. Not many years passed, however, before this view proved to be a bitter delusion. Some said that the Italian bombing of Corfu in 1923 marked the end of the hope for peaceful change. Whether or not that be true, it is certain that the events of 1931, and the years that followed, effectively extinguished any hope in the efficacy of the League system in this present age.

In that year another era of imperialism began. Japan marched into Manchuria as the first step in her effort to gain control of the East and to make effective her "Asiatic Monroe Doctrine." One of the impelling motives behind Japanese aggression was to gain raw materials and markets for her expanding industry. Halted for a time after 1933, Japan instituted a campaign of further expansion in 1937. Her plan seems to have been to gain control in North China before the Chinese Nationalists had an opportunity of consolidating their control over the whole of China. The Japanese found that this consolidation had proceeded farther than they had anticipated; their campaign was thus forced to become more extensive than they had, perhaps, at first intended.

Mussolini, following the Japanese example, conquered Ethopia in 1935-1936, ostensibly in order to secure new markets and an outlet for Italy's surplus population. Taking advantage of the turmoil in Europe resulting from the rape of Ethopia, Hitler moved into the Rhineland. This event marked the ominous beginning of his expansionist program.

After Hitler's absorption of Czechoslovakia, Great Britain became convinced that further German expansion threatened the Empire. The Nazi march into Poland in September, 1939, marked the beginning of World War II.

What was the moving factor in the imperialism of the last quarter of the nineteenth century? What is the cause of the imperialism of the present era? Do both phenomena result from the same or similar causes? The first critical studies of imperialism appeared only about forty years ago. The most thorough study was that of J. A. Hobson, an English liberal critic of capitalism. He may have taken the germ of his argument from a study of imperialism written by an American economist, Charles A. Conant. Both of these men agree that imperialism originated in the general economic *milieu* of the time. Marxian writers have developed the most systematic theory of imperialism, basing their argument on much the same grounds as those stated earlier by Hobson. For the Marxists imperialism is simply a late stage in the development of capitalism. At this stage of capitalistic development savings are greater than can profitably be invested at home; more goods are manufactured than can be disposed of in the ordinarily available market; more raw materials are needed for the manufacture of goods. This being the case, the industrial countries expand their political control over new and undeveloped areas which will afford opportunity for the investment of idle capital, open up new markets, and make necessary raw materials available. In order to protect the home market and the colonial market for the benefit of the industrial capitalists of the state, the government instituted a policy of protective tariffs, thus excluding the products of competing capitalistic states. A protective system becomes, in the Marxian theory, a necessary concomitant of imperialism.

Although the belief that imperialism is economic in its origins has had widespread acceptance among thinkers both Marxian and non-Marxian, within the last few years there has been a decided trend away from the economic interpretation of imperialism. Professor Eugene Staley has made a case study of several examples of imperialism; the results of this study he published in 1935 under the title *War and the Private Investor*. In this book Staley argues that in numerous instances the cause of imperialistic aggression has been political rather than economic. In many cases the governments of the expansionist states desired control over certain areas for political and strategic reasons. In order to further their purpose they encouraged economic and financial interests within their own countries to make investments in the desired areas; later these governments took over the control of the territory they wanted under the pretext of protecting the investments of their nationals.

Two years after the appearance of Staley's work, Professor Rupert Emerson published his *Malaysia*, a critical and meticulous study of British and Dutch imperialism in the Malay States and Netherlands India. Emerson reached the conclusion that imperialism in these areas was a result of political rather than economic factors. He found that generally the political forces ran ahead of the economic forces in the extension of British and Dutch rule. He found in many instances that the colonial governments proceeded contrary to the wishes of the business and commercial groups interested in the exploitation of the controlled areas. This, he believed, resulted in a large measure from the fact that there existed an "ideological and functional distinction" between the economic and the political institutions of the imperialistic states.

These case studies have indicated that the Marxian theory of imperialism is not universally applicable as an explanation of this very important phenomenon. In order, however, to develop a consistent theory of imperialism additional case studies are necessary. This present work is an endeavor to examine the motives and the factors underlying the imperialism of Joseph Chamberlain. Chamberlain was the leader of British imperialism in the 1890's. The factors that influenced the development of his policy of Imperial expansion and consolidation were in all probability those influencing the general movement toward imperialism in this period of British history. As this period of British imperialism ran parallel to similar movements of expansion in France, Russia and Germany, it is perhaps natural to assume that factors influencing the one may have also influenced the others. If there is a continuity of the factors influencing imperial developments in various periods of history, the results of this study may be profitably applied in attempting to explain the present wave of imperialism.

It has been generally assumed by those who advocate an economic interpretation of imperialism that the British imperialism of the late nineteenth century offers splendid proof of their contentions. At that time capitalism was well developed in Great Britain. There was a need for markets in which to dispose of surplus goods and a need for sources of supply for raw materials. Certain other factors deemed necessary to a policy of imperialism were not, however, present. It is generally assumed by those who interpret imperialism in economic terms that a protective tariff is necessary to a policy of imperialism. British imperialism of the late nineteenth century, however, began when England was a free-trade state; this policy of free trade was not replaced by a protective tariff until 1931—after the decline of imperialism in Great Britain. It is also generally held by those who follow the Marxian argument that a policy of expansion is necessary to offer a field of investment for idle capital, yet the peak period of investment of British capital abroad came in the twenty-five years prior to the beginning of the movement for expansion under Disraeli. During the peak period of imperialism the rate of investment of British capital outside of Great Britain suffered a decline.[1] During this period

Great Britain invested more capital in the United States than in her own possessions. Although colonial expansion was to offer new markets for British goods, less than half of the trade of the colonies in this period of expansion was conducted with the mother country. If this is true, then the economic interpretation of imperialism is open to some doubt. A search must be made elsewhere for the factors behind the movement. Since it is in the last decades of the nineteenth century that British imperialism was at its height, a study of that period should be valuable in determining the causes of the phenomenon. Since, moreover, Joseph Chamberlain is considered the leading Imperial statesman of the period, a study of his policies should offer some clues to the factors immediately responsible for the rise of contemporary imperialism.

Mid-nineteenth century England has been characterized as anti-imperialist in its outlook. The feeling was widespread that those colonies which have since become Dominions, should be allowed to go their own way, become autonomous, and even be encouraged to separate from Great Britain entirely. Gladstone was of the opinion that by giving the colonies their freedom Great Britain would be assured of the good-will and affection of the colonies. He advocated giving the colonies control over their tariffs, native policy and waste land.[2] At almost the same time, 1852, Disraeli was writing about "these wretched colonies [which] will all be independent in a few years and [which] are a millstone about our necks."[3] Gladstone remained a Little Englander throughout his career, but Disraeli twenty years later launched a great era of imperialism.

The anti-imperialism of this period was in part a reaction against the centralized control of the colonies so caustically criticized by "The Theorists of 1830," and in part the logical development of the liberal principles of *laissez faire* and free trade. England had long had a tradition of government of the colonies by the Colonial Office. Faith in the wisdom of this method had not been shaken by the American Revolution; that episode made the British Government doubtful of the wisdom of local control. The practice of centralized control had not made for harmony, however. In South Africa, Canada, and Australia constant clashes occurred between the elected representatives and an executive responsible not to the legislature but to the Crown. This disharmony made social, political and economic reform well-nigh impossible. The result was that the natural resources of the colonies remained undeveloped. At this time Lord Durham, Edward Gibbon Wakefield, Charles Buller, and Sir William Molesworth came forward with plans to correct the old system. The *sine qua non* of good colonial government was, to these "Theorists of 1830," local self-government, the executive being responsible to the elected legislature. The local government was to enjoy power over all questions not directly involving the mother country. The Imperial Government ought to interfere as little as possible with the internal affairs of the colonies.

The root principle enunciated by the Colonial Reformers was that the colonies should have responsible government; the argument for the principle was most admirably set forth in Lord Durham's classic report in this connection. He argued that the representatives sent out by the Crown were not competent to judge of the wisdom of colonial legislation since the problems of the colonies were quite different from those of the mother country. Durham believed that the governor should not attempt to direct the activity of the locally elected legislature but should follow the advice of a Ministry responsible to that legislature.

The ideas of the Colonial Reformers regarding responsible government did not meet with the hearty approval of the officials at Whitehall. They feared that if responsible government was conceded the Crown would have no representative in the colonies with power to protect Imperial interests; they also raised objections on the ground that no party system existed in the colonies and therefore it would be well-nigh impossible for responsible government to function. They also thought that a satisfactory division of colonial and Imperial functions was impossible; any division would lead to disputes and quarrels. The Duke of Wellington contended that colonial self-government and the continued sovereignty of the Crown were incompatible. It was probably because of these numerous fears and objections that in the Canadian Act of Union of 1840 nothing was said about conferring responsible government upon the Canadian colonists. In fact, the first governor appointed after the Act of Union said he would do all in his power to put down the idea of responsible government. It was not until the appointment of Lord Elgin, a son-in-law of Lord Durham, that Canada received responsible government—not because of any legislative act but because Lord Elgin followed the recommendations of the Durham report which Downing Street had ignored.

The acceptance of responsible government in Canada by Whitehall in 1849 marked the break-up of the old colonial system. With the adoption of free trade at the same time certain distinct features of the old colonial system, preferential tariffs and the Navigation Acts were doomed to extinction. At the time of the debate on the repeal of the

Corn Laws the opponents of the measure argued that the adoption of free trade would mean the dissolution of the Empire. They argued that the Empire within itself was self-sustaining and that inter-Imperial trade ought to be encouraged. Such a policy would make the Empire well-nigh invincible. The free traders recognized that their policy might result in the dissolution of the Empire, but this fact did not trouble them. They felt that England ought to pursue her own interests, which they identified with universal interests on Utilitarian grounds.

The repeal of the Corn Laws worked a hardship on Canadian wheat growers, who had invested large sums in that industry, when the protected English market became free to all the world. The Canadian revenues declined sharply and the colonists demanded that they be released from the obligation of giving preferential treatment to British goods. In granting this request by an act in 1846, the Imperial Government gave up the principle that the mother country ought to regulate the trade of the colonies. The British Government did not realize the full implication of this grant for some time. It persisted in the belief that it conferred no right upon the colonies to levy their own tariffs; it simply abolished preferential duties in favor of free trade. The attitude was but natural. England adopted free trade and desired the whole world to adopt it, but other countries would be discouraged from adopting such a policy if the British colonies set up protective systems. Soon after the repeal of the Corn Laws and the Navigation Acts, New Brunswick passed a law paying bounties to certain industries; this law the Colonial Office accepted because of the temporary circumstances involved, but it instructed the representative of the Crown to assent to no additional legislation of this character. The Imperial Government also turned a deaf ear to the appeals of Newfoundland for measures to restrict the fishing of American vessels in waters reserved exclusively to British subjects. The British Government made no move to rescue the sugar industry of the West Indies wrecked by the adoption of free trade. It was not until 1855 that Australia acquired the right to levy her own tariffs. In that year the Parliament passed an act setting up colonial self-government in the Australian colonies; one provision of the act granted permission to erect tariff barriers. In 1859 the Colonial Office assented to a Canadian act which provided for a tariff on imported goods. By 1873 the colonies had all adopted protective measures. The wishes of the free traders that their principles should be extended to the colonies were disregarded entirely. However, the Crown Colonies continued under free trade principles.[4]

Those who wrote on colonial affairs in the middle of the century confined their remarks in large part to Canada, Australia, New Zealand, and South Africa, being unconcerned about the colonies of Great Britain which were occupied largely by native races. Charles Dilke was one of the first to devote much attention to these dependencies. Although in his *Greater Britain* he advocated the release of the self-governing colonies, he did not apply the same argument to the other British possessions. He favored the retention of the Crown Colonies and India in order to save them from anarchy and to provide "a nursery for our statesmen and warriors." The English would have been forsaking their duty to civilization if they had not continued their task of governing and educating the native races. Dilke thought that the British were obliged to be trustees for those races unable to cope with the conditions of modern civilization. The widespread popularity of Dilke's work indicated that he had expressed ideas acceptable to large sections of the population.

During the fifties the British Government paid little attention to the colonies; this was in part due to the belief that the self-governing colonies would and should drift away when they became able to govern themselves. It was also due to the prevalence of the Manchesterian views in England. A change in outlook was made possible, however, by the fact that the principles of Liberalism, although widespread, were never accepted by everyone. There was actually in England a dichotomy of views which can best be seen in the lives of Richard Cobden and Lord Palmerston. The Liberalism of Cobden and his associates was a consistent doctrine based on natural laws, operating universally although not evenly, England being farther advanced than other European states. Constitutional government and free trade were a part of this natural plan; when once these facts were apparent to all, peace would ensue. Palmerstonian principles were slightly different. He favored peace because contention obstructed business; he thought constitutional government desirable because absolutism oppressed people and led to strife; he supported free trade because it made for prosperity. But he saw that as long as these principles were not universally accepted clashes of interest between Great Britain and other countries would arise. When these clashes occurred, Palmerston favored a brisk defense of British interests for he believed that the clashes resulted from the impaired vision of his opponents rather than from any fault of his own; he did not rely on the working of the natural law to correct the vision of his opponent but put faith in the British fleet. The universal liberal principles were for Palmerston merely expedients which served the selfish interests of the English. Because of this attitude Cobden cordially hated him, but the average Englishman never bothered to examine the logic of Palmerstonian principles; he held to the liberal principles and supported Palmerston. This was a natural attitude to take; the average man saw that England had advanced beyond Continental Europe in justice, decency, and humanity. He also had an evangelistic fervor to preach the gospel of Liberalism to the less advanced. Palmerston was his missionary.[5]

Because Liberalism did not become firmly rooted in Great Britain, other ideas and other principles were able to come in and displace it. Gladstone, who became Prime Minister in 1868, was the leader of the Liberal Party and one of the staunchest Liberals of his day; yet he sought in religion and in an aristocratic sense of responsibility checks with which to keep Liberalism within bounds. Although this is true of his policy in general, Gladstone must be considered as a "Little Englander" and an anti-imperialist. He advocated a union of the colonies based on sentiment rather than on force. He did not believe that the mother country was justified in interfering in colonial legislation. The problems of the colonies were not parallel to problems in Great Britain, and therefore English customs and laws could not be taken as a safe guide in administering colonial affairs. It was better to allow the colonies to solve their own problems in their own way. While the colonies ought to be given control of their own affairs, Gladstone thought they ought to assume the expense of their own military defense; England ought only to support the naval defense. He thought that if colonies supported their own defense systems they would be more likely to render assistance to the Empire in time of war. Gladstone thought that the unity of the Empire ought to be founded on freedom, good will and affection, for on no other foundation could it withstand destruction. He said, "The colonies ought to be masters in their own households, and their allegiance to the British Crown should be purely voluntary."[6] He looked upon the Empire as satiated and was opposed to the further extension of its boundaries. He stated as his rule on this question that the British Government should "not annex any territory, great or small, without the well understood and expressed wish of the people to be annexed, freely and generously expressed, and authenticated by the best means the case could afford."[7] However, Gladstone failed to abide by this rule at all times; during his administration Great Britain assumed control, direct or indirect, over Griqualand West and the Fiji Islands.

The reaction against Gladstone's anti-imperialistic policy was responsible for the development of the movement towards the "New Imperialism." In 1869 the Gladstone Cabinet was engaged in evacuating Imperial troops from New Zealand in line with a policy laid down by the House of Commons in 1862 and since followed by the Governments of both parties. At this particular time, however, the native Maori tribes had risen and the New Zealanders found difficulty in suppressing the outbreak. They asked that the Imperial troops be allowed to remain in view of the dangerous military situation. This request the Cabinet, acting through the Colonial Secretary, Lord Granville, refused. They likewise refused to grant New Zealand a loan for defense purposes. These events aroused a great deal of attention. The policy of the Government was attacked in both Houses of Parliament and in the press. The belief that the Gladstone Cabinet was on the point of allowing the colonies to go their own way and that their policy toward New Zealand was the first move in that direction led directly to the new imperialist movement.[8]

Soon after the Cabinet refused to grant aid to the New Zealanders, the Colonial Institute was organized. The purpose of this institute was to create an interest in the colonies and the British possessions. Whether due to the activity of the Institute or to the changing intellectual background of the period, a new interest in the colonies and their problems made itself manifest within a short time. It was at this time that the influence of Darwin commenced to be felt. The Darwinian concepts, it was believed, gave scientific proof to the already existing notion of the racial superiority of the British. This had a two-fold effect upon the colonial problem. With reference to the self-governing colonies it gave rise to a desire to preserve the Empire because the colonists were members of the same race. With reference to the other British possessions it gave scholarly proof to the rightness of the British rule over these areas and became a basic argument for the extension of British rule over other races. The British were thus able to find justification for what they felt to be their destiny. Such an attitude of mind was not peculiar to the English. Much the same trend was occurring in France at the same time; the changing intellectual climate gave rise to the French notion of their *mission civilisatrice*.

Disraeli succeeded Gladstone as Prime Minister in 1874. In his earlier years he had been anti-imperialistic along with the rest of his countrymen. In 1852 he spoke of the the colonies as millstones about the neck of England; in 1866 he referred to Canada and South Africa

as "deadweights which we do not govern," and advocated the withdrawal of British troops from these areas.[9] On June 24, 1872, however,
he had taken imperialism under the wing of the Conservative Party
when he proclaimed the three great objects of that party to be the
maintenance of British institutions, the preservation of the Empire, and
social reform. In speaking on the preservation of imperialist policies,
he attempted to blame the Liberals for the continuous effort to dis-
integrate the Empire, forgetting that it was a Liberal, Lord Grey, who
had defended the rights of Whitehall against the colonial claims, and
that it was a Conservative Ministry of which Disraeli was a leading
member that had granted self-government to New Zealand. He ascribed the failure of the efforts for the dismemberment of the Empire
to the strong sympathies of the colonies for the mother country and
declared that in his opinion "no minister in this country will do his
duty who neglects any opportunity of reconstructing as much as possible our colonial Empire, and of responding to those distant sympathies which may become the source of incalculable strength and happiness to this land."[10] Disraeli stated further that the granting of
self-government to the colonies should have been accompanied by a
policy of Imperial consolidation, a military code and an Imperial
council. He would put an end to the Cobdenite principle of non-intervention and restore the prestige of Great Britain by taking an active
part in the settlement of world affairs.

The popularity of this speech—probably a trial balloon—accounted
for the strong policy he pursued. This policy of "Bounce and Bluster"
led to the association of jingoism and imperialism as synonyms. Others
have referred to Disraeli's policy as one of bombastic imperialism in
which the blind extension of the Empire is considered a value in itself.
Disraeli certainly had a flair for displaying the external symbols of
Imperial rule, as was evidenced by his sponsorship of the Royal Titles
Act conferring the title of "Empress of India" upon Queen Victoria.
It has been suggested with some weight that Disraeli had no particular
love for imperialism and that he merely supported it as a policy that
would successfully "dish the Whigs."[11] Undoubtedly politics was an
important factor in shaping Disraeli's policies, but he was probably
sincere in his belief in the value of the extension of the Empire for
its own sake.

In 1880 Gladstone again became Prime Minister but he made
two serious political mistakes. He did not reverse the Disraelian policy
completely, to the disappointment of the old-line Liberals. Nor did

he continue or strengthen the expansionist policy of Disraeli; as a result he lost the support of the imperialists.

When Gladstone formed his Cabinet in 1880 he made Joseph Chamberlain President of the Board of Trade. Chamberlain entered the Cabinet as the leader of the Radicals. He remained a Radical until the introduction of the Home Rule Bill in 1886. The decision he then made to oppose that measure led to his adoption of a policy of imperialism which he pursued to the end of his life, becoming the most influential British Imperial statesman. It is the development of Chamberlain's ideas of imperialism with which this study is concerned.

REFERENCES

[1] W. L. Langer, "A Critique of Imperialism," *Foreign Affairs*, 1935, v. 14, p. 103.

[2] Paul Knaplund, *Gladstone and British Imperial Policy* (London, 1927), 82-86.

[3] W. F. Moneypenny & G. E. Buckle, *The Life of Benjamin Disraeli* (New York, 1910-1920), III, 385.

[4] See C. H. Currey, *British Colonial Policy, 1783-1915* (Oxford, 1916) for a detailed discussion.

[5] See Raymond J. Sontag, *Germany and England* (New York and London 1938), Chapters I and II for a discussion of Cobden and Palmerston.

[6] Knaplund, *op. cit.*, 96.

[7] *Ibid.*, 133.

[8] C. A. Bodelsen, *Studies in Mid-Victorian Imperialism* (London, 1924), 89-94.

[9] Moneypenny and Buckle, *op. cit.*, IV, 476.

[10] *Ibid.*, V, 195.

[11] Cf. Bodelsen, *op. cit.*, 124.

Chamberlain's Background

If it had been suggested in 1876, the year that Joseph Chamberlain entered Parliament, that a short quarter of a century later he would be the leading spokesman of British imperialism, England's citizenry would certainly have been surprised if not astounded, for at that time he was fighting for Free Schools, Free Church, and Free Lands and was fast becoming the leader of British Radicals. His rise to political fame had been meteoric. Born in London, July 8, 1836, of a well-to-do middle-class family, he had been educated privately and in University College School, then a stronghold of the Unitarian faith. After completing his formal education with some distinction, he entered his father's business—shoe-making. But he did not long continue in this trade; he was soon to go to Birmingham, and there begin his career.

The circumstances which resulted in this change are these: Uncle J. S. Nettleford, who lived in Birmingham, was engaged in the making of screws. In 1851 certain American patents were displayed in London which foretold a revolution in that particular industry. Nettleford saw that if others bought these patents his business might be forced to the wall, but he had not sufficient funds to buy the patent rights and make the necessary changes in his establishment. He appealed to his brother-in-law, the London shoe-maker, to advance a portion of the necessary 30,000 pounds; the latter agreed to make the advance with the stipulation that his son, Joseph, then eighteen, go to Birmingham to protect the Chamberlain interests in the business. So in 1854 young Chamberlain departed for Birmingham. For the next ten or twelve years he was chiefly interested in his uncle's enterprise; yet he had sufficient time to devote himself to the activities of the Edgbaston Debating Society and to teach Sunday-school classes in the Unitarian Church.

But it was not long before Joseph Chamberlain's energies were to be turned to the service of social reform. A new Reform Bill passed by the Disraeli Government was soon to enfranchise a host of first voters. Even those of strong Liberal sentiments were worried about the problem that this raised, for the newly enfranchised voters were in a large measure illiterate. Great Britain had been slow to provide public education. Elementary schools were maintained by the Church of England for those who could pay the required fees; there was no widespread system of schools supported out of the public purse. Chamberlain and his friends decided that if the extension of the franchise was to be justified it was necessary to provide broader opportunities for education; this decision resulted in the formation of the Birmingham Educational Society, an organization in which Joseph Chamberlain took a leading role. The first task of this society was to make a survey of the educational needs of the city; the results showing that less than half of the children in the city attended schools of any sort. But the survey also impressed Chamberlain in another way; he became aware of the appalling conditions existing in the slums of Birmingham: the filth of the unpaved streets, the crowded, unsanitary, and otherwise inadequate housing facilites, and the lack of a sufficient supply of pure water. These discoveries led to his entry into politics.

It soon became apparent to the Birmingham Educational Society that the problem would remain unsolved unless national legislation was passed. Hence the formation of a national educational society was in order; this society had as its guiding principles free and compulsory erucation of a non-sectarian character. The natural outcome was Chamberlain's later fight for the disestablishment of the Church. The society became so influential in the next year that in 1870 the Government in power introduced an Education Bill, but it was not to the liking of Chamberlain's group; Gladstone was too devoted to the Church to consent to the idea of nonsectarian education. Chamberlain and a delegation went to London to plead their case to no avail; the measure was passed, giving the local school boards the optional right to extend aid to the denominational schools already in existence rather than setting up public schools where no religious tests were applicable. But even though defeated, Chamberlain's group intended to make the best use possible of the law as passed and to continue the fight. A tactical mistake in the campaign for the election of the school board in Birmingham, the stronghold of the group, led to the winning of a majority of the fifteen seats by the "Beer and Bible" Tories, but they did not hold their majority for long and even while they held it their actions were hampered by the refusal of the Birmingham Town Council, controlled by Chamberlainites, to grant the necessary funds to be given to the denominational schools. By 1873 the Radicals had control of Birmingham's School Board and were able in the years that followed to set up a model educational system for the nation at large.

The implications of education for the masses were evident to Joseph Chamberlain and he was not slow to call them to the attention of the public. He pointed out that educated workers would no longer be content and would no longer be compelled to work at the then current wages; education would bring in its wake a strong labor movement. Moreover, the agricultural laborer would be affected; the whole English land system would have to be revised. From this he developed his program of Free Schools, Free Church, Free Land, and Free Labor, which he elaborated in an article in the *Fortnightly Review,* an article in which he did not spare the feelings of the Whigs or the other Liberal leaders. Soon after, in 1874, he made his first Parliamentary fight in the city of Sheffield, where he was destined to be defeated by the "Beer and Bible" alliance.

As has been indicated, the initial survey of education in Birmingham had impressed upon Chamberlain the deplorable slum conditions, which, as he readily saw, were the cause of much of the petty and even gross crime of the city. As far as the policies of the Tories and the old Liberals toward these problems were concerned, there was little to choose from between the two. The Tories were antagonistic to reform and the *laissez-faire* attitude of the Liberals was hardly less so. The Liberals of Birmingham, however, were differently inclined. Chamberlain had been on the Town Council since 1869; by 1873 he had become its leader and he was selected as the Radical candidate for Mayor. That the vigorous forces of local Liberalism won in that election was due in a large part to the yeoman service of Schnadhorst and the "caucus," or the introduction of machine politics. Having won, Chamberlain set out to make the best of his opportunities.

The first year in office resulted in the purchase by the city of the gas works in order that the lighting system of the city should become a municipal matter. In the next year Birmingham acquired control of the water supply, which formerly had been a source of sickness and disease. The privately owned water company had supplied water to its pipes only three days of the week; for the remainder surface wells, with all their attendant pollutions, were used. The lighting and water services once in the city's hands, Chamberlain launched a large-scale slum clearance program designed to make decent dwellings out of areas that were, as he said, "unfit for a dog to die in." His program was quite successful—to judge by vital statistics indicating a sharp fall in the death rate and a general decrease in illness.

Chamberlain's efforts in connection with the extension of education and Birmingham's municipal reforms had attracted wide attention and he soon became the leader of the Radical wing of the Liberals of the country much the same as Charles Dilke had become its leader in Parliament. In 1876, George Dixon, one of the three Parliamentary representatives from Birmingham retired after a long period of service and was succeeded by Chamberlain. Having once entered Parliament, however, Chamberlain found that he could do little to influence legislation of a reformative nature; the Eastern Crisis had forced domestic politics into the background. At this time he organized the National Liberal Federation and disseminated information on his "caucus" methods—information which proved to be of inestimable help to the Liberals in the General Election of 1880. Recognition of his aid in the election was extended when Gladstone made him President of the Board of Trade in his new Cabinet.

As President of the Board of Trade, Chamberlain's duties and activities covered a wide range, including supervision of foreign and domestic commerce, domestic business practices, and patent rights. Although the Gladstone Cabinet, as the Disraeli Cabinet before it, forced domestic questions into the background because of the exigencies of foreign and Imperial questions, Chamberlain succeeded in introducing and passing some much needed legislation, notably an Employers' Liability Act, a Seamen's Wages Act (intended to protect sailors from loan sharks), a Bankruptcy Act which became the model of all future legislation, and a Patents Act liberalizing the granting of patent rights. His most important bill had to be withdrawn at the insistence of the Chambers of Commerce, ship owners, and other owners of capital. He had discovered, as a result of an investigation urged by a fellow-member of Parliament, that certain ship owners sent unseaworthy but heavily insured ships to sea with the intent that they should founder and thereby make the insurance payable. As a necessary part of such happenings, the crews lost their lives. Aroused by the results of his investigation, Chamberlain introduced his Merchants Shipping Bill to correct the situation, but too many members of Parliament had interest in the shipping business or had pressure put upon them by those who did. The result was that Chamberlain withdrew the measure at the request of the Cabinet. Years later his ideas became the law but the incident left him embittered at the time.

While checked in the Cabinet, Chamberlain was active in the country, where he was intent on campaigning for manhood suffrage, equal electoral districts, and payment of members of Parliament; to this program the diffident Whigs objected while the Tories looked on with alarm. In 1884, the Cabinet introduced a Franchise Bill to extend the suffrage to about 2,000,000 additional persons; this Bill passed the Commons, but was rejected by the Lords—which caused Gladstone to recess Parliament in order to appeal to the country under the slogan, "The Peers against the people." In such a campaign Chamberlain was at his best; he attacked the House of Lords with considerable vigor, drawing rather acrid replies from Lord Salisbury, with whom he was later to lead the Conservative Party. Chamberlain and Salisbury were enemies at this time; in the summer of 1884 they invited each other to lead their followers in a head-cracking melée in Hyde Park. Although Chamberlain's speeches were perhaps untactful in some instances, he captured the enthusiasm of the young Liberals. Lloyd George spoke of him as one who understood the masses and would probably be the future leader of the Liberal Party.[1] The Liberal campaign carried the day and when Parliament reconvened in the fall, the Lords accepted the Franchise Bill with minor changes. The country was not to wait long for a demonstration of the effects of such an extension of the suffrage. The Cabinet soon found itself torn with dissension over an Irish Land Bill which was rejected by the Commons in June of the following year. The Tories took control but remained in office only a brief period.

In the autumn the election for which Chamberlain had been waiting took place. He had actually begun his campaign the previous summer with a number of speeches; indeed other preparations had been made prior to that. For two years a series of articles outlining a Radical policy had been running in the *Fortnightly Review;* these were reprinted at this time in book form as *The Radical Programme.* When the campaign began in 1885, Chamberlain made a tour of Great Britain, speaking emphatically in favor of free primary education, full local government for the counties, financial reform through graduated taxation other than income taxes, land reform to give the agricultural laborer the opportunity to own his own farm, manhood suffrage, and the disestablishment of the Church. It was certainly due to his strenuous campaign efforts that the Liberals polled as large a vote as they did, but they did not have a majority in Parliament, the Irish members holding the decisive vote with their compact body of eighty-six. This fact forced the Cabinet, in Gladstone's estimation, to consider the Irish question before all others, a decision displeasing to Chamberlain, who had thought that the campaign of 1885 was the beginning of a widespread movement of social reform. Differences with the Cabinet on this matter led to his resignation and ultimately to a fundamental change in his policy, but this must be reserved for more extended treatment later.[2]

Enough has been said of the early career of Joseph Chamberlain to indicate that he was primarily concerned with local affairs. He took great pride in this fact, as is indicated by the following statement to his fellow-townsmen:

"I am so parochially minded that I look with greater satisfaction to our annexation of the gas and water, to our scientific frontier in the improvement area, than I do to the results of that Imperial policy which has given us Cyprus and the Transvaal; and I am prouder of having been engaged with you in warring against ignorance and disease and crime in Birmingham, than if I had been the author of the Zulu war or had instigated the invasion of Afghanistan."[3]

Had it not been for the antagonisms developed as a result of the Irish Question, Joseph Chamberlain might have distinguished himself as the leader of a great English reform movement instead of becoming the leader of British Imperialism.

In attempting to formulate a statement of Joseph Chamberlain's theory of imperialism or to marshal his ideas on the subject, it is necessary to keep in mind always the fact that these ideas developed slowly over a period of years. He did not begin his public career with any well-formulated beliefs concerning British Imperial policy. It is therefore necessary to state his theory in terms of chronological development. In doing this, the author has made every effort to avoid overlapping other studies in the field. His object has been to use historical material to illustrate the germination of Chamberlain's ideas, the transition from one position to another, and the fruition of ripened thought.

Even in the early days, when Chamberlain was primarily concerned with social reform, he was not entirely unmindful of the world beyond England or of the problems confronting the Empire. As early as 1858 he tilted with that thorough-going pacifist, John Bright. In the previous year Birmingham had returned Bright to Parliament. After the election, Bright outlined his position to his constituents, strongly opposing the intervention of Great Britain in the affairs of any other country or people. At a meeting of the local Edgbaston Debating Society held after this event, Chamberlain, then twenty-two, expressed himself as being considerably opposed to Bright's policy of non-intervention and peace at any price. In the course of his remarks, young Chamberlain contended that the aristocracy was not to blame for all wars, that the wars since 1688 were demanded by the people, that the world was an unsafe place, and it was necessary to be prepared at all times.[4] J. L. Garvin, the biographer of Chamberlain, regards this incident as pointing an index-finger to the future Imperial statesman, but certainly there is a difference in being unwilling to support a position of complete pacifism and in being willing to support a policy of large-scale Imperial expansion. One can regard this statement as indicative of a future course only if in the future development of Chamberlain's ideas a consistent trend toward imperialism can be proved.

Chamberlain hardly concerned himself with Imperial affairs until he entered Parliament in 1876. There, of course, his chief interest was in domestic questions. Other questions undoubtedly thrust themselves upon him in the ordinary course of his participation in the tactics of Her Majesty's Opposition. Later, his entry into Gladstone's Cabinet compelled him to become conversant with the Imperial policy of Great Britain in order that he might take part in Cabinet discussions of related matters. His tutors in this field were his friends John Morley and Charles Dilke, whom he had met in connection with his educational reform efforts. He was in constant touch with these men either through letters or personal conversation. It was not until he had met Charles Dilke in 1870[5] that he read the latter's *Greater Britain,* which had appeared some years before. He read Professor Seeley's *The Expansion of England* upon its appearance in 1883. It is said that he sent his son, Austen, to Cambridge because Seeley taught there.[6] One cannot be sure, however, that he sent his son there because Seeley was the author of *The Expansion of England.* Professor Seeley was already well-known and respected in England for his other works, particularly his *Ecce Homo,* which was an attempt to demonstrate the rational basis of religion. Such a concept was undoubtedly welcomed by such a staunch Unitarian as Joseph Chamberlain and might well have influenced him to send his son to study under the author.

Chamberlain's early notions on imperialism were given expression in his letters to John Morley. Writing on December 19, 1875 with regard to the purchase of the Suez Canal shares by the Disraeli Government, he said, "It may or may not be desirable that we should have a finger in the Egyptian pie. But we have got it, and that is the point of view from which the purchase ought to be regarded."[7] A few days later he expressed concern about India, pointing out that the British were in a difficult position "in India and other half-civilized communities"; he did not, however, explain what he considered to be the nature of the difficulty. The duty of the Liberals he thought to be to impress the people with certain definite principles of conduct and to use the errors of the existing Government as opportunities "to preach our doctrines."[8] Morley seemed to think that Chamberlain was becoming particularly interested in India's problems and suggested that the member from Birmingham might well be a future Secretary of State for India. But Chamberlain replied, "I don't think I should like India. I am not cosmopolitan, and should prefer to try my hand on England."[9] He was still intent on domestic reform, which was his first love.

Speaking in the House of Commons in May of 1877, he put himself on record against British intervention in Egypt to safeguard trade. He thought that intervention for such a purpose was selfish and unworthy of the British Empire. However, he admitted that intervention might be necessary to safeguard India, "whose happiness lay in the continued security of our rule."[10] Later in the same year he voted against the annexation of the Transvaal, thus expressing his disapproval of the strong policy of Benjamin Disraeli. The next year he expressed his opinion of the Disraelian policy in strong terms. Lord Lytton, the Indian Viceroy, had involved Britain in a war with Afghanistan over the enforced reception of a British Mission to the Emir. Writing to Morley on October 15, 1878, Chamberlain severely criticized the government. He pointed out the necessity of demonstrating to the electorate the fact that the Afghan War "is the natural consequences of Jingoism, Imperialism, 'British interests' and all the other phrasing of the mountebank government." Moreover, the war was "in perfect harmony with the acquisition of Cyprus and the protectorate of Asia Minor; and it is perhaps fortunate that before going further in the latter bargain we should have here a practical specimen of the sort of work we have so lightly undertaken."[11] Writing to Dilke a few months later he stated that the Liberals must "din into the constituencies that the Government policy is one of *continual*, petty, fruitless, unnecessary and inglorious squabbles."[12]

The Zulu War came in for its share of criticism also; Chamberlain characterized it "as iniquitous and unjust as any in which this country has been engaged."[13] He accused the Government of "recklessly forcing on a war." While he admitted the Cabinet itself might not have wanted this particular war, the New Imperialism enunciated by that body had its effect on the minds and judgments of the "men on the spot." Parliament and the people had the duty to check this spirit—else "there could hardly be a limit to the responsibilities which might be fastened upon us, and none to the difficulties and even disasters yet in store for this country."[14] Continuing his criticisms at a later date, he protested against any possible annexations as a result of the Zulu War, saying that such a policy went against the wishes of the people and of Parliament.[15] With a wealth of illustrative material he raised his voice against the policy of the Government in dealing with the African native population in terms of disguised slavery. He opposed the notion, which he said was current in Africa at the time, that natives might be killed as a sport comparable to hunting big game.[16]

Thus one sees that from the time he actively entered English political life until the time he took office in Gladstone's Cabinet, Chamberlain expressed himself in strong terms as an opponent of the New Imperialism. He was willing to defend the existing Empire but was dead-set against any further acquisitions. One must remember, however, that during this period he was a member of the Opposition; as such he could be quite free in his criticism of the Government. The responsibilities of office might cause him to modify his views. When in office one may be forced to choose between the lesser and the greater evil, while out of office one can always point toward the highest good.

When Gladstone took office in 1880, Chamberlain became, as has been noted, President of the Board of Trade. One of the first questions that forced itself upon the attention of the new Government was the matter of the Transvaal. Should Britain retrocede this territory to the Boers or continue to hold it? The relations between the Britons and the Boers had been none too cordial for the past half century or more. Formerly the Boers had settled in the Cape Colony from whence they had moved across the Vaal in the Great Trek of 1836, which culminated from several grievances of the Boers against the British Government. For one thing the British had not paid the Boers as much as they had promised for their slaves when slavery was abolished in 1833; again, the Boers did not think the British had given them sufficient protection from the Kaffirs in the years that followed. Once in the new country, the Boers established a republic, the independence of which was recognized by Great Britain in the Sand River Convention of 1852. So matters stood when Disraeli appointed as his Secretary of State for the Colonies, Lord Carnarvon, who dreamed of a South African Confederation and had sent Sir Theophilus Shepstone to the Transvaal to enlist the Boers in the realization of his dream. Sir Theophilus carried with him a document empowering him to annex the country to Great Britain if

he found the population willing; this he did. In April of 1877 he proclaimed the Transvaal to be British territory, promising self-government and allowing the Boer officials to remain in office to act for
the British Government. Oom Paul Kruger and other Boer officials
journeyed to London to protest the action, but there they were only
given assurances that they would be allowed to govern themselves.
With the election of Gladstone, Kruger and the Boers hoped for a
change in policy.

The Transvaal matter came up for discussion in the Cabinet in
May, 1880, soon after it had taken office. At this time Chamberlain
declared himself in favor of a complete reversal of the Disraelian
policy, which he thought the Cabinet was in duty bound to do since
the national elections had indicated that the country was heartily
opposed to Disraeli's actions. He noted in his private "Memorandum"
that he was the only member of the Cabinet who took this forthright
stand.[17] Although the other Cabinet members were opposed to the
Disraelian policy, they hesitated to go so far as to reverse it completely. Before coming to a final decision, the Cabinet examined the
reports from the British officials in the Transvaal and decided that
since it appeared that taxes were being collected without objections
and that the Boers appeared peacefully inclined, British rule was
not irksome. Moreover, the testimony of Sir Bartle Frere and Lord
Wolseley indicated that civil strife might ensue should the British
withdraw.[18] Therefore, the Gladstone Government retained the Transvaal, selecting Chamberlain to defend the policy before Parliament
on August 31, 1881. In addition to outlining the reasons impelling the
Cabinet to take the course it had decided upon, Chamberlain pointed
out that an immediate decision had been necessary because of fear
of the evil which might result froma policy of indecision.[19]

In view of Chamberlain's earlier desire to repudiate the Disraelian
policy entirely, one wonders at his being chosen by the Cabinet to defend the retention of the Transvaal. The reasons for the choice do not
appear in the available documents. It may be possible, however, that
the Cabinet thought it wise to select him in order to put him on record
publicly as being in accord with Cabinet policy. Thus, it could tie
his hands with respect to future decisions on the Transvaal, thereby
preventing him from taking a stand in opposition to that of the
Cabinet.

However,the decision to retain the Transvaal did not close the
question. The Boers had pinned their faith on Gladstone's probable
reversal of the annexation and were bitterly disappointed when this

did not occur. They might have accepted the situation had Gladstone made any efforts toward setting up local institutions to the liking of the inhabitants or had he consulted the wishes of the Boers. Instead, he allowed the Disraelian officials in the Transvaal to continue in office along with the old policies. Having failed to receive what they considered to be justice from the hands of Gladstone, the Boers soon took matters into their own hands. The refusal of one of their number, Bezeidenhut, to pay taxes brought united support from his neighbors, preventing the revenue officers from taking his property in lieu of payment. Open rebellion soon followed, in the course of which General Colley and quite a few British soldiers were slain at Majuba Hill. It would have been possible for the British to conquer the Boers and overrun the territory, but the fact that the Cabinet had decided to retain the territory with some misgivings prompted it to authorize negotiations for peace rather than a punitive mission. This policy received the support of Chamberlain; he considered the rebellion a direct result of the Government's failure to return the Transvaal at the first opportunity. He did not see the necessity for avenging the "insult" to the flag at Majuba. He thought that in this case Britain was the aggressor, not the Boers. To him the fact that British soldiers died at Majuba did not make their aggression any the less noticeable. Since Great Britain was a great and powerful nation, it was in a position to admit that it had erred; no shame could attach to such an admission; but should it continue with an aggressive policy it would be guilty of wilful wrongdoing in the "vain pursuit of military glory."[20]

Chamberlain could not see that the retrocession of the Transvaal involved dismemberment of the Empire in any sense. After all, the territory had been annexed only a scant three years previously, following assurances that the majority of the white inhabitants really desired it—assurances strikingly disproved by the events culminating in the British fiasco at Majuba. At the time of the annexation, the Disraeli Government had also declared that unless the Transvaal came under British rule the British would be confronted with native wars; nevertheless the Zulu War and another with Secocoeni had occurred. The assumptions incident to the annexation had all been proved false. Why then continue to act on them? If the Government intended to rule the Boers it would be necessary to maintain at least 20,000 British troops in an area occupied by some 40,000 Boers who looked to their co-religionists of the Orange Free State for sympathy and aid in time of urgent need.[21] If such a large force were needed to preserve order, free representative local institutions were out of the question. The governmental administration of the Transvaal would necessarily have to become despotic. If Great Britain attempted to rule the Boers despotically, it would subject itself to embarrassing relations with the Cape Dutch; this might force the British to increase the number of troops in the Cape Colony in order to preserve peace. From a materialistic point of view such a procedure was unwise as it did not seem likely that the Boers would pay into the Treasury much more than 100,000 pounds annually. But Chamberlain thought that considerations other than monetary compelled Britain to return the Transvaal. Great Britain was bound by the Sand River Convention to guarantee the independence of the Boers and not to extend control west of the Vaal River. This Convention could not be ignored without the consent of the Boers. At the time of the annexation in 1877 the British Government had thought the Boers willing, but now the honor of Great Britain demanded that the Transvaal be returned.[22]

That was Chamberlain's public stand. Privately he confessed that he looked toward the future with certain apprehensions. He felt certain that Britain had pursued the right course in dealing with the Boers after Majuba, but he saw that conditions were such that the future of the British and the Boers might be strained. Writing, in the fall of 1882, to his friend, Dr. R. W. Dale, he said:

"The circumstances attending the surrender of the Transvaal have no doubt given the Boers an excessive opinion of their power. In the event of a new conflict they would probably secure the assistance of the Orange Free State, and the sympathy of the Dutch and possibly Germany . . . I should be reluctant to press matters to the utmost [war?] unless it became necessary; and even then I should feel the gravest anxiety as to the result."[23]

Previously, Chamberlain had written to Gladstone, "Unless some unforseen circumstances lead to a large immigration of Englishmen into the Transvaal, I believe the Boers will, sooner or later, worry this country into granting their independence."[24] But the Boers did not receive complete independence under the terms of the London Convention. In addition to the restrictions placed on their political independence, they were required to respect the rights of the native population at their borders. These stipulations the Boers disregarded; soon after signing the Convention, they declared a protectorate over Bechuanaland and attacked chiefs Makoroane and Montsioa. Chamberlain sprang to the defense of the natives. He informed the Cabinet that Britain could not escape its responsibility to the natives and urged that the British forces in South Africa be immediately augmented in order to carry out this responsibility.[25] As a result of his insistence

Sir Charles Warren was instructed to proceed at once to Bechuana-land and restore the chiefs.

It is necessary at this point to draw some distinctions respecting Joseph Chamberlain's imperialism during the period under review. His attitude toward the question of the annexation of the Transvaal was in accordance with the general principles of Liberalism at the time. The policies of aggression of the Disraeli Government (which he hoped would never occur again in British history[26]) were contrary to current Liberal thought. John Stuart Mill had warned the British people several decades before that it was impossible for one people justly to govern another; in every attempt to do this one people had inevitably been exploited by the other.

The general principles of Liberalism were, of course, suffering a severe attack at this time. The establishment of the German and Italian nations had not led to the general spread of Liberalism as the Liberals of the Frankfort Convention and the followers of Mazzini had hoped. Instead Bismark developed his ideas of *Realpolitik,* which became, to a certain extent, the model for other states. International rivalries had become rather bitter by this time. The French were motivated by a desire to revenge Sedan; the Germans were preparing to prevent such a step; Italy still looked to the recovery of *Italia irridenta;* England and Germany had just begun their trade rivalry, which was also to bring on naval rivalry. The thought patterns of the time were also undergoing a change. Darwin's biological discoveries had opened up new vistas of speculation. Darwin himself had warned against the application of his biological principles to the field of social and political relationships but his advice had gone unheeded, for the supporters of the idea of "Might makes right" thought they had found scientific support for their contentions. Progress, they believed, was the result of conflict in which the strongest were the victors. One ought not to interfere in this conflict, nor ought one to sympathize with the weak lest a desire to preserve be the result, thus interfering with natural processes. It was these false theories that the Liberals, led by Gladstone, attempted in vain to overthrow.

During the Boer crisis of 1880-1881 Chamberlain supported the Liberals and even became one of their leaders; he passed over to the other side later. The Transvaal had been taken in violation of the creed of Liberalism; Majuba had shown the mistake of the Liberals in not returning it at the first opportunity. In advocating its return, Chamberlain was not unmindful of the prestige of Great Britain, although his interpretation of this idea differed from the general imperialist doctrine. While the imperialist thought that prestige should be enhanced by pursuing a policy which *mutatis mutandis* would have been considered "bullying" if carried on by one individual against another, Chamberlain believed that the prestige of Great Britain would benefit by admitting a mistake and in dealing fairly with others. As will appear later, however, he was not unmindful of the necessity of maintaining British prestige in the case of Egypt, which may indicate that one of the main reasons Chamberlain was willing to see the Transvaal returned was the fact that it was unimportant at that time. No considerations of increased British trade could have influenced the policy. Moreover, it was not in this instance necessary to maintain British prestige as against the expansion of other powers; the German-Boer ties had not been forged at this time.

The relation of "civilized" and "backward" races is fraught with many difficulties. Too often Europeans feel that their superior culture can be transferred to the natives with the same celerity with which women's fashions are changed—and with as little harm. The truth of the matter is that the natives lose their frame of reference in the change if it is too sudden and doubts arise regarding the benefits which are thus derived from European civilization. Into this picture enters, also, the relative merits of various nations as colonizers. The British, on the whole, thought themselves well fitted for the task, although this was not necessarily a universal belief. This idea of the superiority of British colonization methods had led the British to make certain guarantees to the Bechuana chiefs, which guarantees had been violated by the Boers. Chamberlain, probably influenced by the idea of British superiority and also by considerations for the welfare of the natives, took a firm stand against the Boer policy toward the natives; within twenty years the natives would be longing for the return of Boer rule, *i. e.*, after the effects of Chamberlain's colonial policy had been felt in the aftermath of the Boer War, but that is another story.

Another angle of Chamberlain's imperialism developed as a result of the possibility of declaring a protectorate over New Guinea. He agreed that Great Britain had no right to prevent other nations from colonizing the unappropriated portions of the earth's surface. It was impossible to anticipate foreign nations by declaring a universal protectorate over all "backward" areas.[27] But that he would like to have done so was apparent from his note to Charles Dilke in December, 1884:

"I don't care the least about New Guinea and I am not afraid of German colonization, but I don't like to be checked by Bismarck or anyone else, and I should let Bismarck know that if he is finally resolved to be unfriendly we accept the position and will pay him out when ever the opportunity arises."[28]

A few days later he wrote Dilke that he favored taking Zululand in order to anticipate Germany there, but that Gladstone had objected.[29] In this respect he was following one of the stock arguments of the imperialists. So long as other nations were interested in expansion it was necessary for Great Britain to take what she could get in order to maintain her position in European affairs. It seemed obligatory to "run with the pack." The notion that what appeared hurtful to one's neighbor was helpful to one's self became prevalent.

The imperial question which gave Chamberlain most concern during his first term of office in the Cabinet related to British intervention in Egypt. At first he showed his sympathy with the plight of the fellaheen and the possibilities of reform latent in the Arabi rebellion. On January 7, 1882, he summarized his view in the Cabinet:

"Extortion was practiced on a large scale and in every department of the Government. The unfortunate fellaheen were burthened with excessive taxation rendered more onerous by the arbitrary way in which it was collected. Public works were suffered to get into disrepair and even the system of irrigation, on which the life of the country depends, was allowed to fall into the greatest disorder.

"My view was that we had not sufficient information to appreciate properly the so-called revolutionary movement. It might be the legitimate expression of discontent and of resistance to oppression. If so, it ought to be guided and not repressed."[30]

This statement was not at all imperialistic. Chamberlain was but showing the sympathy that all nineteenth century Liberals had for revolutionary movements, having as their object the extension of Liberal principles. Nineteenth century Liberals had as one of their basic tenets the spread of the democratic principle or the extension of the right of self-government. To this end they had supported the revolutions of 1830 and of 1848, and also the revolutions in Germany and Italy in the sixties, although in these two instances Liberal principles had not been triumphant to the degree hoped for. The Liberals did not limit their sympathy for the extension of popular control to Western Europe; they lent their aid to the Greeks in their struggle against the Turks and it was natural that they should also wish for their extension in Egypt.

Great Britain and France had intervened in Egypt under a system of dual control. Their intervention resulted from the failure of the Khedive to meet the interest on the loans which he had negotiated with the powers. It is not illogical to assume that the Powers made these loans knowing that the Khedive would not meet his obligations. The Khedive having defaulted, the Powers used the situation as an excuse to take over control of the country—a distinct asset to England as a further safeguard for the line of Empire leading to India, and to both France and England for the protection of the Suez Canal. Whatever may have been the actual reasons for intervention, the Powers attempted to make their action less obnoxious by declaring that the reason for interference was to rehabilitate the financial and other administrative agencies of the Egyptian Government. They had not interfered with the military establishment, however, leaving that as a problem to be settled by the Egyptian and Turkish officials. Under the leadership of Arabi Pasha, the army had attempted to induce the Egyptian authorities to inaugurate certain military reforms; when this failed the army took matters into their own hands. Arabi at first paid no attention to the incipient nationalist movement but with the outbreak of revolt the two forces naturally coalesced. This nationalist movement, as is generally true of all such movements in their early stages, was intensely anti-foreign, being directed against the Turkish officials and the Europeans.

The actions of Arabi following the course of anti-foreign incidents caused Chamberlain to alter his former view of the revolutionists. On June 11, 1882, the populace of Alexandria rioted, several Europeans were killed, and the British consul was injured. From this date Chamberlain was for "active measures." The fact that British blood had been spilled aroused his ire. Arabi was now only a "military adventurer" interested in increasing the size and pay of the army; bankruptcy and anarchy would follow if he succeeded. At the same time, however, Chamberlain was intent on keeping the claims of the bondholders separate from such reasons for intervention as protection of the route to India and reparation for the massacre.[31] Besides, he had not lost his concern for the interests of the fellaheen. On June 21 he induced the Cabinet to adopt his position that intervention for the purpose of imposing restrictions on the right of the Egyptians to manage their own affairs would be unwise. He felt that if the latter preferred their own system, even though corrupt, England had no right to impose another system even though corruption might be extirpated thereby. "Intervention should be directed not to impose on Egypt institutions of our choice but to secure for the Egyptian people a free choice for themselves so far as this may not be inconsistent with the permanent interests of other powers."[32] This, with the exceptions of the last clause, is certainly anti-imperialistic. The fact that the rights of the Egyptians were to be subordinated to the interests of the other powers, however, could certainly be utilized by the imperialists to advantage.

Meanwhile discussion in the Cabinet centered on whether or not the British fleet lying off Alexandria should be ordered to stop Arabi —by force if warnings went unheeded. Beauchamp-Seymour, the commander there, had asked the Cabinet for permission to do this. In mid-June the Cabinet granted its permission. What was Chamberlain's stand on this point? John Bright, his colleague from Birmingham, thought he was directly responsible.[33] Bright resigned from the Cabinet after the bombardment; being a pacifist he could hardly have done otherwise. Another of Chamberlain's associates in the Ministry, Lord Granville, wrote of the Cabinet decision, "We had several cabinets more or less formal about Egypt. Bright of course, the most peaceable, Chamberlain almost the greatest Jingo."[34] Garvin is of the opinion that this is an inaccurate statement,[35] but the opinion of Bright and Granville cannot be dismissed as of no worth. It will be necessary to carry the story further before a final judgment can be made.

But even though Chamberlain might have been intent on seeking vengeance for the British blood that had been spiled on foreign soil, he did not lose sight of the interests of the Egyptian masses. In October he pointed out to the Cabinet how easy it was to pass over the obligation to aid the Egyptians in the establishment of representative institutions. He reminded his colleagues that ruling classes had always denied the fitness of the masses for representative institutions, indicating that he did not consider the argument valid as a general rule or when used with reference to the Egyptians. At the same time he reiterated his desire to keep the interests of the bondholders separate and apart from the other reasons for intervention; he stood by his opinion that they should receive no more consideration than bondholders who held obligations against stable governments.[36] Writing to Dilke shortly thereafter, he expressed fear lest the fine phrases for which the war was supposedly fought "develop the institution," "promote liberties," and "Egypt for the Egyptians" would be forgotten in the interests of finance.[37] But, had he not done his part to remove the validity from these phrases when he urged the bombardment of Alexandria? How did he reconcile that with a desire to leave Egypt to the Egyptians?

He had at first been sympathetic to the revolutionaries because he hoped that popular government would be extended thereby, but the moment that British and other European citizens had been endangered he had taken steps that finally resulted in the suppression of the revolution. His desire for the extension of Liberal principles seemed to have been subordinated to his pride in the British race. In formulating a policy for British action in Egypt, Chamberlain seems not to have made the distinctions between rulers and ruled which he was then wont to make in advocating domestic reform. In the latter connection he had advocated the extension of suffrage to the masses in order to turn out the ruling classes in Great Britain, his basic assumption being that no one class or fraction had any inherent right to rule another class. By a natural extension of this line of reasoning one might come to the conclusion that Great Britain had no right to rule the Egyptians. The Egyptians were trying to organize a government which would be more concerned for the general welfare; but Great Britain (the ruling class) wanted to prevent the Egyptians (the masses) from doing so. It so happened that the first to agitate for intervention in Egypt were the bondholders, who in general represented the ruling classes in Great Britain which Chamberlain had fought. In supporting a policy of intervention, he came to help those whom he wished to depose while hindering the logical development of self-government. The national aspirations of the Egyptians naturally brought them into conflict with England because of its intervention policy. Chamberlain did not seem to view the question as one between rulers and ruled, but as one between a dominant and a backward race in which the weaker must be taught its rightful place. Whenever the Liberal principle of self-determination came into conflict with the "rights" of British citizens, he leaned to the support of the latter rather than the former. National prestige and competition with other European nations for territory and influence undoubtedly played a part in determining this attitude.

Late in December Chamberlain spoke at Ashton-under-Lyne in defense of the Government's actions in Egypt and in support of his position:

"I can say for myself that I have always protested in the strongest terms against the policy of non-intervention or peace at any price, which I have believed to be an unworthy and ignoble doctrine for any great nation to hold. I have always thought that a great nation like an individual had duties and responsibilities to its neighbors, and that it could not wrap itself up in a policy of selfish isolation and say that nothing concerned it unless its material interests were directly attacked."[38]

Several days after this speech, John Bright wrote Chamberlain that the arguments used in his speech were the stock arguments of the Jingo school that he had heard in Parliament for forty years; they were the words used by Palmerston in his "mischievous career" and had been used to defend all the crimes which had wasted the blood and wealth of Great Britain.[39] Perhaps Lord Granville had not been far wrong in his estimate of Chamberlain.

In his "Memorandum" written early in 1883 Chamberlain summarized his views on intervention in Egypt. He believed that intervention was unpopular with the majority of the Liberal party and that Bright could have destroyed the Government had he made public speeches against its policy. A general notion existed that the might of Great Britain had been used to protect the Egyptian bondholders. All enthusiasm for British victories was allayed by the marked superiority of the British forces. While Chamberlain had not agreed with the Radicals on the question of intervention he was in favor of evacuation within a short period; he believed that the objects for which the policy of intervention had been adopted would be acomplished in at least two years.[40] In March of the same year he wrote to John Morley, elaborating on what he considered necessary to accomplish in Egypt before Great Britain could evacuate the territory:

"We cannot leave anarchy behind us, and we have to see that our interference has produced some real benefits for the Egyptian people but when we have established the best institutions for guaranteeing their liberties and securing the administration of justice which the circumstances of the case permit, we shall have discharged our obligations and rights, and shall then be entitled to leave Egypt to the Egyptians."[41]

There is no reason to doubt Chamberlain's sincerity in believing that the lot of the Egyptian masses would be bettered by reason of British intervention, or that intervention was, as he said, "the least of all the evils of which they [the Government] had to choose."[42] The difficulty arises in attempting to decide whether or not he was or was not an imperialist in this instance. Even assuming that he did not intend to be, the line separating his position from that of the rabid imperialists is all too subtly drawn. Who is to judge what are the "best institutions?" Who shall say when "real benefits" have been conferred? The road leading to permanent occupancy had been opened.

Although the road was open, Chamberlain apparently did not relish travelling it. He was eager for Great Britain to acomplish its purpose in Egypt and withdraw, but circumstances worked against this. In January of 1884 he had to admit that an epidemic of cholera in Egypt and Egyptian reverses in the Sudan conspired to delay the fulfilment of British objectives; he did not want this to be used as an excuse for making the occupation permanent, however. He was not eager for the extension of the Empire simply to make it larger. Yet he wanted Britain to stay until it had fulfilled the assurances given at the time of intervention; he was confident that these plans would "with time, patience and discretion, succeed, and be completely accomplished."[43] He did not want to stay permanently, yet he wanted to stay long enough to accomplish certain purposes; but reform proceeds so slowly and progress cannot always be recognized in short periods.

In all the excitement over the sending of General Gordon to the Sudan, Chamberlain saw a move to force Great Britain to declare Egypt a protectorate, which would lead later to annexation. He wrote his friend J. T. Bunce, editor of *The Birmingham Daily Post*, that this meant a guarantee for the debts of the bondholders—which he opposed.[44] And yet, after Gordon's fall, Chamberlain became Jingoistic in a sense. John Morley desired that Britain should retire from Egypt after this event, but Chamberlain demurred. British honor must be avenged. Englishmen must not die unnoticed. "We must retake Khartoum even if we leave it again immediately," he wrote. Yet he added characteristically, "I am ready to protest and resign if necessary rather than commit myself to any permanent occupancy, or war of conquest properly so called."[45]

The policy of intervention in Egypt which Chamberlain was backing was not entirely acceptable to the other European Powers interested in forcing the Egyptian Government to pay the debts which it had contracted. But these Powers could come to no agreement as to a solution of the matter. After the failure of the conference of the Powers early in August, 1884, Chamberlain suggested that a possible solution might be to provide some international guarantee for the neutrality of Egypt, as had been done in the case of Belgium. The Powers would, under such an agreement, accept joint responsibility for the administrative reform of the country. This would relieve Great Britain of the responsibility it had undertaken when it entered Egypt, while guaranteeing that the purpose it had in intervening would be fulfilled.[46] But the Cabinet did not seem able to agree on any settled policy. It was practically impossible to make an agreement that would have satisfied all the powers. The French were particularly insistent that the Egyptian debts be paid. As Chamberlain had been anxious to declare protectorates over Zululand and New Guinea to thwart Germany, so now he was desirous of taking a strong line in Egypt to circumvent the French. Harcourt recorded in his diary that Chamberlain was "very Jingo on the Egyptian question." Later— January 20, 1885—he went to see Chamberlain at a time he was suffering from toothache. Chamberlain told Harcourt that no doubt the peace-at-any-price group were glad that he would miss the Cabinet meeting on account of his tooth since his absence assured them of having their own way.[47]

Garvin is of the opinion that this does not represent the real view of Joseph Chamberlain. His contention is that Chamberlain in private conversation was given to light repartee and persiflage and that his remarks ought not to be given much weight.[48] But Garvin, a little later, quotes a letter which Chamberlain wrote to Harcourt in which he says, "So the peace-at-any-price party will have it all their own way. If I were there I should be for telling the French to go to the devil."[49] This is not a conversation, but Garvin explains it away by saying that Chamberlain was racked with pain, hence this statement also ought to be discounted. One is tempted to ask, however, whether a person in great suffering would have gone to the trouble to write a letter if he did not feel strongly on the subjects he discussed. If this were an isolated incident it might be disregarded, but it has been seen above that Lord Granville and John Bright had with some justification accused Chamberlain of being jingoistic with reference to the Egyptian question.

Neither Chamberlain nor the others in the Cabinet received in the end what they desired. In March, 1885, they reached a compromise by which France and Great Britain jointly guaranteed a loan to Egypt which stipulated that the two Powers should, acting together, reform the financial structure of the country. This agreement Chamberlain defended in Parliament as being advantageous to the Egyptian taxpayer and the government. He was quick to point out that it conferred on England no new right of interference nor any further title to political or financial control.[50]

In summarizing Chamberlain's view on imperialism in this early period it is evident that his ideas on domestic reform colored his policy with reference to Imperial questions. He was interested in the welfare of the masses and in the spread of Liberal principles, hence he wanted to assist the Egyptians, through British intervention, to attain those ends. This also influenced him, in his concern for the natives of South Africa. In regard to Egypt he was probably moved by other considerations. While he may have sympathized with those who favored non-intervention, he thought that the interests of Great Britain were so widespread that it was impossible to remain separate and apart. It was necessary to give some attention to "the honour and the interests"[51] of England. Since Egypt guarded the route to India it was not possible to allow "another Power to take up a preponderating position there."[52] Five months later—November 18, 1885—however, he was saying "that all our troubles in Egypt, aye, and all our troubles in Ireland, all resulted from that unfortunate and miserable five years of vigorous policy abroad . . . from 1874 to 1880."[53] From what has been seen above, however, one gathers that Chamberlain had become slightly tarred by the same pitch as he was an advocate of a "strong policy" in certain instances. It is rather difficult to characterize his policy in regard to Egypt. As he admitted to his friend Dilke, "It is awfully difficult work steering between Jingoism and peace at any price."[54] Perhaps it is best to agree with him and say that he was attempting to take the middle course. In doing so, however, he came rather close to the jingo line. The testimony of Lord Granville, William Vernon Harcourt, and John Bright bear witness to the truth of this. Perhaps one of the reasons he came so close to being a jingo was the fact that his anger was aroused the instant he thought any foreign nation was interfering in affairs tinged with English interests. Witness his attitude toward Germany over New Guinea and Zululand and toward France over Egypt.

Another matter that seemed to arouse his ire was the shedding of British blood. He wanted to bombard Alexandria after the riots; he wanted to retake Khartoum after Gordon's fall, even though the British were to retire immediately thereafter. In both instances he seemed to desire to repay an insult to "British honor." One wonders that he did not want to avenge the British after Majuba Hill. The answer lies, perhaps, in the fact that his desire to bombard Alexandria and to retake Khartoum was bound up with his desire to preserve the integrity of the route to India and to prevent other nations from intervening in Egyptian affairs. The Transvaal was in 1881 rather unimportant and Chamberlain had put himself on record as being of the opinion that the British were the aggressors in that instance.[55] No other nation appeared interested in the Transvaal at this time; hence Chamberlain's penchant for favoring a strong policy to circumvent other nations could not exercise itself.

In the light of future developments in Chamberlain's career it is interesting to note that he devoted little attention to the relation of trade to these Imperial questions. His remarks on trade during this period were all in defense of free trade and in condemnation of Protection.

REFERENCES

[1] J. Hugh Edwards, *David Lloyd George, The Man and the Statesman* (New York, 1929), I, 75-6.

[2] Except where credit is otherwise given, the material for these remarks on Chamberlain's life was gathered from J. L. Garvin, *The Life of Joseph Chamberlain* (New York & London, 1932-4), I, II. A full treatment of his social reforms may be found in Elsie Elizabeth Gulley, *Joseph Chamberlain and Social Reform* (New York, 1928).

[3] Charles W. Boyd (ed.), *Mr. Chamberlain's Speeches* (London, 1914), I, 77.

[4] N. Murrell Marris, *The Right Hon. J. Chamberlain, The Man and the Statesman* (London, 1900), 48; also in Garvin, *op.cit.*, I, 60.

[5] *Ibid.*, 122.

[6] *Ibid.*, 494.

[7] Garvin, *op. cit.*, 223.

[8] *Ibid.*

[9] *Ibid.*, 224.

[10] *Hansard's Parliamentary Debates*, 3rd Series, v. 234, p. 453.

[11] Quoted in Garvin, *op. cit.*, 267.

[12] Quoted *ibid.*

[13] *Ibid.*, 269.

[14] *Hansard*, 3rd Series, v. 244, pp. 1814-6, March 27, 1879.

[15] *Ibid.*, v. 246, p. 1387, May 27, 1879.

[16] *Ibid.*, v. 248, pp. 1854-72.

[17] Garvin, *op. cit.*, I, 313.

[18] Speech in Birmingham, June 7, 1881, in Henry W. Lucy (ed.), *Speeches of the Right Hon. J. Chamberlain* (London, 1885), 19; also *Hansard*, 3rd Series, v. 263, p. 1819.

[19] *Ibid.*, 3rd Series, v. 256, p. 908, also v. 278, pp. 231-43.

[20] Lucy, *op.cit.*, 21.

[21] *Ibid.*, 16-18.

[22] *Hansard*, 3rd Series, v. 263, 1817-1831.

[23] Quoted in Garvin, *op. cit.*, I, 490.

[24] Quoted, *ibid.*, 439.

[25] Chamberlain's minute to the Cabinet of January 10, 1884 quoted *ibid.*, 492.

[26] Lucy, *op. cit.*, 16.

[27] Boyd, *op. cit.*, I, 136.

[28] Quoted in Garvin, *op. cit.*, I, 538.

[29] *Ibid.*, 538.

[30] Chamberlain's "Memorandum" quoted *ibid.*, 445.

[31] *Ibid.*, 446-7.

[32] *Ibid.*, 448.

[33] *Ibid.*, 449.

[34] E. G. P.–F. Fitzmaurice, *The Life of Granville George Leverson Gower, Lord Granville* (New York and London, 1905), II, 265.

[35] Garvin, *op. cit.*, 449.

[36] *Ibid.*, 451.

[37] *Ibid.*, 452.

[38] Quoted in *The Times*, December 20, 1882.

39*Vide* Garvin, *op cit.*, 454, for the full contents of the letter.
40*Ibid.*, 456.
41Quoted, *ibid.*, 500-1.
42Speech at Newcastle-on-tyne, January 15, 1884, Lucy, *op. cit.*, 69.
43*Ibid.*, 70.
44Garvin, *op. cit.*, 517.
45*Ibid.*, 528.
46*Ibid.*, 522.
47A. G. Gardiner, *The Life of Sir William Harcourt* (London, 1923), I, 514.
48Garvin, *op. cit.*, 537.
49*Ibid.*, 539.
50*Hansard*, 3rd Series, v. 296, pp. 876-7, March 27, 1885.
51Lucy, *op. cit.*, 139.
52*Ibid.*, 140.
53Quoted in *The Times*, November 19, 1885.
54Garvin, *op. cit.*, 542.
55Lucy, *op. cit.*, 21.

The Swing Toward Imperialism

Ireland had long been a thorn in the flesh of English politics. The memories of the Irish were long and they looked upon the wrongs inflicted by the Cromwellian and other conquests not as mere history but as events that happened yesterday; their resentment did not cool with the passage of time. Admittedly, the Irish had grievances. With the exception of Belfast and the surrounding territory, Ireland was an agricutural country whose fertility was none too great; every agricultural slump intensified the misery of the tenants. The situation was not bettered because of the fact that many land owners were Englishmen not living in Ireland or the descendants of those who had been given land by the English Crown at the time of the conquest of Ireland. Coupled with this was the fact that the peasantry was militantly Catholic while the landlords were Protestants. Even had this not been so the ordinary grievances of the tenants were numerous. They had no security of tenure of their land; the rents were not certain, leading to the practice of rack-renting; the landlord left improvements to the tenant but did not pay for these improvements when the tenant left.

The political and economic grievances of the Irish resulted in agitation for the repeal of the Union with Great Britain which had been declared in 1800. The term "Home Rule" was coined by Isaac Butt in 1870 as being less offensive than "Repeal." During the following few years Butt was the leader of the Irish party in Parliament. In the late seventies he was pushed aside by Charles Stewart Parnell. The tactic of obstruction was developed and used by Parnell as a means of bringing the Irish grievances to the attention of Parliament. During 1879 he kept the Commons in session for two entire nights—events that caused a sensation. Obstruction was not the only method by which Parliament's attention became centered on Ireland. The agricultural crisis which occurred about the time Parnell began his obstructionist tactics in the House of Commons brought violence in its wake. The Irish Republican Brotherhood, assisted by the Clan-na-Gael, its American counterpart, and the Fenians, began the policy of

37

cattle maiming, house burning, threats of death, and, before long, assassination itself. With the organization of the Irish Land League under the presidency of Parnell, the Parliamentary representatives indicated their approval of this procedure although they had held aloof at first. During the course of the campaign of violence a new word found its way into the English language and a new and powerful political weapon was forged. Parnell, in September, 1880, had urged that anyone taking a farm from which a tenant had been evicted should be shunned "as a leper of old." The first person to take such a farm was a certain Captain Boycott; though the man himself has long since been forgotten, his name still lives. Once begun, the terrorist activities of the Irish increased in violence and at times were beyond the control of the Irish leaders; the policy thus pursued antagonized many Englishmen who might have been otherwise sympathetic and probably had much to do with the postponement of the success of Home Rule, although the question of disruption of the Empire played a major part in this delay.

During the whole period of the Irish controversy, which marked the turning point in his career, Joseph Chamberlain remained of one mind: he was against separation. He first publicly expressed this opinion in this unsuccessful stand for the Sheffield constituency. On January 1, 1874, he stated his position:

"I believe the extension of the system of local government would be of the greatest advantage both to England and to Ireland. But it is only fair to add that I am not in favour of any system which would go further than this, and which would separate the imperial relations which at present exist between the two countries."[1]

Garvin is of the opinion that Chamberlain had indicated his opposition to Irish Home Rule as early as 1870 in a private letter.[2] In this letter to his friend George Dixon, Chamberlain, in discussing the Education Bill of 1870, had said:

"It [the Bill] is not National Education at all—it is a trick to strengthen the Church of England against the Liberation Society and to pave the way for the *one* concession to Ireland which no English Parliament ought to make, and which, when made, will only prepare for that repeal of the Union which I expect must come sooner or later."[3]

Chamberlain did not explain what the "*one* concession" was, but in saying that it would lead to repeal he did not add that he was opposed to such a step; he merely indicated that he believed repeal would come in the course of time; there is no word to indicate that he was either in favor of or against the measure. He was opposed to the concession that would lead up to it, but the fact that in the same sentence he postulated the inevitability of repeal leads one to infer that his opposition to the concession proceeded from other reasons than the mere fact that it would lead to repeal, which was due in any case. His public statement in 1874 was clearly in opposition to separation—not so the letter to Dixon.

Up until the time the Gladstone Government came into power in 1880, Chamberlain gave little attention to formulating a policy or outlining his ideas on Irish reform. Toward the end of Disraeli's term of office he wrote Morley that he had been thinking of a plan for modified Home Rule. In his "Memorandum" he noted that "a wise and liberal policy of reform would do much to conciliate the Irish people and render powerless the efforts of political agitators."[4]

When the Gladstone Cabinet took office in 1880, the agitation over agrarian unrest had reached a point demanding immediate attention. Unfortunately the act allowing the Government to coerce the tenants was about to expire, which meant that the ordinary laws would soon be restored; no doubt the Disraeli Government had intended that this should be so. Quick action on reform measures was necessary if the Government was to avoid embarrassment, for only through whole-hearted efforts to redress the grievances of the Irish could trouble be avoided. When Forster, the new Chief Secretary, went to Dublin Castle to take charge, the permanent officials there urged upon him the necessity of renewing the coercion bills; the Cabinet refused to grant this authority, however, introducing instead a Compensation for Disturbances Bill intended to ameliorate the lot of the tenants harshly evicted. Passed by the House of Commons, this bill met defeat at the hands of the stubborn Lords. Forster now wanted to introduce coercive legislation immediately. To this Chamberlain was violently opposed, writing to Gladstone that he would have to resign if such a policy was pursued.[5] He wanted the Government to give some evidence of its desire to ameliorate the condition of the Irish tenantry before coercion was again renewed; the complaints seemed to him to be based on reasonable grievances which ought to be remedied before attempting to crush the natural expression of dissatisfaction. To have done otherwise would have been similar to an attempt to cure smallpox by treating the postules. He agreed to remain in the Cabinet only if a Land Bill was introduced together with a suspension of evictions for the interim between the introduction of the Land Bill and its final passage. Gladstone consented to this and a measure embodying fair rent, free sale and fixity of tenure was forthcoming, passing both houses successfully by August, 1881.

In explaining his support of coercion to his constituents on June 7, 1881, Chamberlain stated that he was opposed to the idea of coercion, but that the disorder had to be put down; he emphasized that the Government was not only merely interested in quieting the disorder but that it was chiefly interested in redress of grievances, which would be accomplished by the new Land Bill. Since the Government had shown its intentions he was hopeful that the Irish would cease their violent actions although he realized that Parnell and his associates desired something more than a redress of grievances, namely separation, while the Government was interested in seeing Ireland become as much a part of the Empire as was Scotland in fact as well as in name. [6] As time passed, however, Chamberlain became more and more convinced of the necessity of coercion on an increasing scale; yet he was uneasy about the whole matter. He believed that the Land League had done a good work in rousing the tenants against the tyranny of their landlords. At the same time he realized that the application of coercion meant the struggle of two opposing despotisms, the one a despotism designed to restore constitutional order, the other intended "to subvert law and produce anarchy as a precedent to revolutionary changes." [7] Since he desired to restore the constitutional order he felt that coercion, if necessary to this end, was justifiable. But means and ends are often confused when one people attempts to force its will upon another; constitutionalism maintained by the sword may cease to be constitutionalism. Force used to stifle disorder arising out of unbearable conditions results in renewed grievances which require more force in order that "the law" may be preserved, too often to the detriment of ordinary liberties. When armed force is used, as Laski has reminded us:

"The innocent not less than the guilty are its victims. It is the enemy of Reason and Freedom—the twin goddesses whose triumph gives what of beauty there is in the ultimate texture of men's lives. Where there is social conflict, there also Hate and Fear rule the destinies of us all; and even if there is high purpose in the price they exact, it is a purpose stained by bloody sacrifice." [8]

John Stuart Mill pointed out that rebellions against ill-usage might be cured by concessions, but that if not cured they become rebellions for an idea of independence in which the individual grievances played but a minor role since, even if redressed, the idea remained. By continuing the policy of coercion the Gladstone Government was hastening the day when a mere redress of grievances would not be sufficient to satisfy the Irish. In attempting to find justification for his position Chamberlain read Mill's pamphlet, *England and Ireland;* he wrote Morley that his position would not have been objectionable to Mill as a passage in the pamphlet met the situation exactly.[9] But there Mill was discussing the necessity of maintaining the union because of the geographical position of the two islands. It is rather difficult to see that Mill was justifying a policy of coercion in this instance as the purpose of the pamphlet—the central argument running through it—was to show the necessity of Irish reform if England was to continue to rule there.[10]

Mill's pamphlet evidently influenced Chamberlain a great deal for in many of his later speeches his schemes for Irish reform show a striking similarity to those of the great Utilitarian. In his speech at Liverpool, October 25, 1881, he repeated Mill's warning against the advisability of separation, saying that the weight of the necessary military expenditures incident to independence would crush Ireland. Separation at a time when so much bitter feeling existed would not heal the breach but would leave cause for future quarrels. Taking the Civil War in the United States as an illustration, Chamberlain declared that union must be preserved and pointed out to the Irish:

"there is nothing which you may not ask and hope to obtain—equal laws, equal justice, equal opportunity, equal prosperity. These shall be freely accorded to you, your wishes shall be our guide, your prejudices shall be by us respected, your interests shall be our interests, but nature and your position have forged insoluble links, which cannot be sundered without being fraught with consequences of misery and ruin to both our countries, and we will use all the resources of the Empire to keep them intact."[11]

The importance of this statement lies in the fact that here Chamberlain nailed his colors to the mast for the public to see. He and Gladstone were the only two members of the Cabinet who had grasped the central issue involved in the Irish question[12]—the necessity for drastic economic reforms. Both were fairly well agreed on this, but Gladstone's mind was still open on the matter of separation; not so Chamberlain's, as he indicated at Liverpool. This was a stand which Gladstone—no doubt—regretted.

Chamberlain was adamant, however; his sensitive nature had been aroused by the Irish proceedings. Having once decided upon a course he was intent on carrying it out regardless of consequences—although he admitted that the Irish had many practical grievances. As he said to Morley, "We are in a state of war, and I will use every conceivable means to come out victorious."[13] Something in Chamberlain's character would brook no opposition. We have seen how he became incensed over the desire of Germany to enter the lists as a colonial competitor and how he desired to tell the French "to go to the devil." As has been said by L. J. Hammond,[14] he would stand "No nonsense" from anyone who stood in his way, be it the Church, the Peers, Ireland, or the Boers. A war was in progress and Chamberlain had enlisted for the duration thereof.

Whatever may have impelled Chamberlain to take his position, no one can accuse him of having taken it without considering the question at great length. He had formulated a policy of his own for reform in Ireland which, he thought, would make separation as unnecessary as he considered it unwise. This plan[15] provided for a great program of public works. Ireland was too poor to finance such a program as he envisioned, hence English capital would be supplied. As Chamberlain had carried through a vast improvement scheme for his home city, Birmingham, so he thought Ireland would benefit from state aid to public works of all kinds, the improvement of communications, aid to industry, the reclamation of land, etc. This, however, was not the whole of his program. In his opinion the seat of all the Irish difficulties arose from agrarian unrest.[16] Before the conquest the Irish were unaccustomed to the idea of absolute rights of property in land, which they never accepted at the hands of the English. Chamberlain desired to establish a system more in line with the Irishman's concept of justice. To do this the landlords would have to be deprived of their rights to eject tenants upon the termination of the lease; the tenants must be given fixity of tenure. Also, the tenants would have to be assured of a property interest in the improvements which they put on the land which they leased and they would have to be assured of fixed rents in lieu of the existing variable ones. Moreover, there was need for the abolition of excessive arrears in rent. After these reforms had been initiated, Chamberlain believed that a system of local government could give the Irish control over their affairs, which was, in general, similar to Gladstone's proposals for local government. Here, again, in these proposals one finds striking resemblance to the proposals made by Mill in 1868.[17]

In 1882 Chamberlain began his role as intermediary between Parnell and the Cabinet, Parnell acting through Captain O'Shea. There is little in this correspondence throwing any light on Chamberlain's ideas concerning Ireland that is not already known. It did, however, provide an opportunity for Chamberlain to become acquainted with several of the Irish leaders, who considered him sympathetic to their cause. These associations led many to expect that Gladstone would appoint Chamberlain as Chief Secretary for Ireland when Forster retired, but Gladstone chose Cavendish instead. After the Phoenix Park murders Gladstone again passed over Chamberlain in selecting a successor to the late Chief Secretary.

Several factors probably influenced Gladstone in ignoring Chamberlain as a possible Irish Chief Secretary. A few weeks before Forster resigned John Morley, through the columns of *The Pall Mall Gazette,* had suggested Chamberlain as the logical successor. Chamberlain often spoke to the public through Morley an dmany thought that Chamberlain was suggesting himself for the office; although nothing of the sort occurred in this instance, Gladstone may have felt that pressure was being applied to name Chamberlain and he refused to respond to such pressure. Gladstone probably looked doubtfully at certain aspects of Chamberlain's social program and was inclined to appoint someone more in accord with his own views. Chamberlain, however, would have been an excellent choice. Although he did not know Ireland at first hand, he sympathized with the plight of the peasants and was sufficiently interested in reform to have studied the needs of the country intently. He also possessed the confidence of the Irish leaders, a fact which would have helped immensely in the settlement of the difficulties. He would have gone to Ireland with a program of action and would have drastically revised the so-called Dublin Castle system based on coercion. His appointment also would have strengthened Gladstone in the Cabinet and might ultimately have prevented Chamberlain's withdrawal from the Cabinet in 1886. That is to say, had Gladstone seen fit to call on Chamberlain for aid in this instance instead of playing a lone hand he might have dispelled some of Chamberlain's later aversion to Gladstone's Home Rule Scheme, which was almost exclusively the product of Gladstone's mind.[18]

After the Phoenix Park murders, the Irish question demanded considerable attention from the Cabinet and Parliament but little was really accomplished due to the inability of the Cabinet to work together on some common policy, the obstructionist tactics of the Parnellites, and the opposition of the Lords. The years 1883 and 1884 have been referred to as "the two lost years" when nothing was done for Ireland. During this time Chamberlain indicated his disapproval of the system by which Ireland was governed—a military system[19] founded on bayonets under which no Irishman could move without being confronted by a representative of a foreign authority, nor were the Irish allowed any voice in local affairs. Under such conditions it was not surprising that the English were regarded with aversion. The chief blame for this state of affairs rested upon the House of Lords,[20] which had resisted all attempts at reform. (Not many years later Chamberlain was to praise the Lords for their action in throwing out the Second Home Rule Bill.) He was seeking a safe middle ground between separation and

"that excessive centralization . . . which throws upon the English Parliament and English officials the duty and burden of supervising every petty detail of Irish affairs, which stifles the national life, which destroys the sense of responsibility, which keeps the people in ignorance of the duties and functions of government, and which produces a perpetual feeling of irritation while it obstructs all the necessary legislation."[21]

In order to give Ireland a decent administration it was necessary, in Chamberlain's opinion, "to reform altogether the absurd and irritating anachronism known as Dublin Castle, to sweep away altogether these alien boards of foreign officials, and to substitute for them a genuine Irish administration for purely Irish business."[22]

During the course of the campaign of 1885 Chamberlain objected to the Parnell program on the ground that it demanded greater powers be given to Ireland than were possessed by any state in the United States, which had always been the model for Irish reform.[23] He outlined what he considered to be the only adequate solution of the Irish difficulties in a letter to Labouchere late in February; in this letter he provided for an arrangement similar to the Federal-State relationship which exists in the United States, including:

"1. Separate legislation for England, Scotland, Wales, and possibly Ulster. The three other Irish provinces might combine.
"2. Imperial legislature at Westminster for Foreign and Colonial Affairs, Army, Navy, Post Office and Customs.
"3. A Supreme Court to arbitrate on respective limits of authority."[24]

The outcome of the election of 1885 had its peculiar features, the Liberals having gained 86 more votes than were held by their Conservative opponents. This gave Parnell sufficient votes to make or break the party in power since he could swing the block of Irish votes—also numbering 86—either way. Parnell probably influenced the size of the Conservative vote for he had at the last moment—after the balloting had been in progress two or three days—ordered the Irish people living in England to vote the Conservative ticket, which they did, being a well-disciplined group. The towns had voted against Gladstone perhaps because of the Gladstonian foreign and Imperial policy, while the counties supported him trusting in the "unauthorized programme" which Chamberlain preached. Gladstone might have been able to have changed the results of the election had he announced what his Irish program was, but he did not do this, feeling that such a policy might be looked upon as a plan to buy votes.

Not long after the election, however, Gladstone indicated to both Parnell and the leaders of the Conservative party that should Salisbury propose an adequate settlement of Irish difficulties supported by Parnell that he would give his suport to the measure. Parnell, always interested in securing the greatest possible concessions to Ireland, decided that the Liberal pasture was the greener and therefore broke with the Conservatives. In January, 1886, on a motion of Jesse Collins, the Government was defeated and Gladstone was commissioned to form a Cabinet.

During this time Gladstone had not indicated at all what he considered to be an "adequate settlement" of the Irish question; he had kept his own counsel, leaving his associates in complete ignorance as to his real plans. Partly this was due to his age; he did not consider that their advice was necessary, perhaps even thinking that they were youthfully presumptious in assuming that it was. Also, he had been absorbed with the Irish question since the organization of his Cabinet of 1881 and felt himself adequate to the situation without the aid of others. But certain associates—particularly Chamberlain—were not so sure that Gladstone was right. He feared that Gladstone had already decided on separation, to which he was unalterably opposed; therefore he refused to join the Cabinet until Gladstone had given him written assurance that he should retain "unlimited liberty of judgment and rejection" on Irish matters.[25]

Even that assurance did not make his entry into the Cabinet easy. Gladstone first offered him the Admiralty, but the Radical in him declined since that was one of the great spending departments. This offer having been refused, Gladstone asked which office Chamberlain desired. Upon receiving Chamberlain's answer that he wanted the Colonies, Gladstone dismissed the suggestion with a curt, "Oh! A Secretary of State!"[26] Not wanting to return to the Board of Trade, Chamberlain had to content himself with the Presidency of the Local Government Board.

The conditions of his entry into the Cabinet are interesting, particularly in the light of future developments. Why did he desire the

Colonial Office- Dilke, who records the incident, does not clarify this question. We have already noted that, although Chamberlain was chiefly interested in social reform at this time, he had concerned himself with Imperial questions and had shown himself tinged with Jingoism in one or two instances—but that seems hardly sufficient reason for his desiring the Colonial Office. A little over a year before, *The Pall Mall Gazette* had published an interview with Merriam, an ex-Cabinet member from the Cape Colony, expressing surprise over Chamberlain's attitude toward Bechuanaland and indicating that he thought that Chamberlain would make a suitable Colonial Secretary.[27] Did this influence his thinking? Perhaps, but it is often easy to see a causal relationship on the basis of *post hoc ergo propter hoc* when in reality the prior event had no relation to that which happened later. Considering that he had just recently campaigned for the "unauthorized programme" one wonders why he did not desire a Cabinet post devoted exclusively to domestic affairs.

Whatever may have been Chamberlain's reasons for desiring the Colonial Office one may wonder why Gladstone was so curt in his refusal. That he was having his trials in the formation of a Cabinet there can be no doubt; he was not the only elderly person in British politics whose feelings had to be considered. The Queen had informed him earlier that she would not accept Granville in the Foreign Office again. It was Gladstone's sad duty to convey this intelligence to his friend (he had sat with him in ten cabinets) and to attempt to console him with the Colonial Office. For that reason the Colonial Office may have been a sore subject with Gladstone at the time of his conversation with Chamberlain.

As the new President of the Local Government Board, Chamberlain felt, however, that Gladstone had been less than courteous to him and his sense of injustice increased over what he assumed to be an additional slight. Gladstone had decided that 600 pounds of the budget might be saved by cutting down salaries of several lesser officials in the Government, one of whom happened to be Chamberlain's *alter ego,* Jesse Collins. Chamberlain protested against this cut, which was restored after much quibbling.[28] He felt that Gladstone was displaying gross ingratitude for the help which both he and Collins had been to the Prime Minister in the recent elections.

Perhaps it is true that this was so. Gladstone may have felt that the "unauthorized programme" had little to do with the outcome of the election. Perhaps he thought that the prestige of the Liberals and the fame of the name of Gladstone were the major factors in the election and that the Radicals in the party were not nearly so strong as they thought they were. That being the case, he may have thought that it was more desirable to gather the Whig elements of the party closer about him. As events later showed, however, the Whigs were as much opposed to his Irish program as was Chamberlain. Had he been more conciliatory to the Birmingham Radical some compromise between the two on the Irish Question might have been worked out.

In reviewing this matter one can not leave out of account the trials and tribulations which Chamberlain had caused the aging Gladstone. While Chamberlain was waging his battle for the "unauthorized programme," his speeches were fiery and provocative. Gladstone received angry demands from the Queen that Chamberlain be silenced; similar suggestions came from cautious members of his own party. In all these cases Gladstone defended his Birmingham colleague; however, he did not necessarily agree with him. No doubt he had been rather irritated by Chamberlain's independence. Nerves had been frayed on both sides, a fact of which neither seemed aware. One may have been too old to recognize his guilt; the other was too stubborn to admit it.

Once in the Cabinet, Chamberlain began work on a local government bill. In the meanwhile, Gladstone was working on his Irish proposals, mostly alone, although he asked others for their advice and was quite cordial to Chamberlain for his suggestions. He would not, however, reveal what was really in his mind. Rumors of various sorts were in circulation indicating that Gladstone would report in favor of separation.

At last, on March 13, the Cabinet learned that he had in mind a vast land purchase scheme to be financed by British credit to the extent of 120,000,000 pounds. His proposal for Irish government included a separate Parliament for Ireland with power to deal with all Irish affairs. Not being able (in the light of his previous decision) to agree with this, Chamberlain sent in his resignation on March 15, basing it on opposition to Irish Home Rule and a land bill designed to make separation possible.[29] Gladstone requested that he defer his decision on the ground that he had presented only a rough draft to the Cabinet, the details not yet being ready. Chamberlain agreed and stayed on until March 26, when Gladstone informed the Cabinet that he thought the simplest manner to deal with Home Rule was to propose a resolution establishing a separate Parliament to deal with purely Irish matters. Upon being informed that Gladstone intended this resolution to indicate that Irish representation at St. Stephens was to cease, that the Irish Parliament would have the custom and excise taxation, the power to establish an Irish judiciary, and all powers not specifically excluded by the enabling act, Chamberlain left the Cabinet accompanied by Trevelyan.[30]

In the light of what Chamberlain had proposed to Labouchere as a solution for the Irish difficulties it might appear that he was resigning over a very few minor differences. He had indicated his support for a separate legislative body for Ireland. However, Gladstone's proposal went farther than he intended his local legislation to go. Chamberlain visioned a legislative body, subordinate in every way to Westminster; he was opposed to Gladstone's plan because it seemed to organize a co-equal legislature at Dublin and more or less terminated Imperial supremacy. In Chamberlain's estimation Imperial supremacy was further threatened by the provisions which gave Ireland control of all taxation and of the judiciary. Chamberlain was willing to concede Ireland a status similar to that which an American state bears to the Federal system; considering that Gladstone's proposals went beyond this, he resigned.

From all accounts by the Cabinet members Gladstone made no move to deter Chamberlain from leaving. He possibly considered that Chamberlain would resign sooner or later over this particular question so that there was no necessity of trying to hold him longer. Chamberlain, for his part, perhaps, thought that Gladstone was seeking to push his social program overboard, using the Irish difficulties as an excuse. Stories circulated in political circles at that time indicated that Chamberlain broke with Gladstone because of dissatisfaction with Gladstone's attitude toward his social program and his displeasure at having to take the Cabinet office of lowest rank.[31] Certainly Harcourt seemed to believe this. In a conversation he had with Chamberlain just before the vote on the second reading of the Home Rule Bill, Harcourt said, "'Now, my dear Chamberlain, confess that no concession whatever would satisfy you, or moderate your hatred of Mr. G., whom you mean to destroy if you can.' Chamberlain would not admit this but denied it with a bad grace."[32] Later he wrote to Granville saying that Chamberlain's motto was *"delenda est Harwarden,* and . . . [he] will have peace at no price."[33] To be sure, Chamberlain was angry with Gladstone for the reasons which Harcourt mentioned and this played some part in his decision to leave the Cabinet. However, Chamberlain sincerely believed that the unity of the Empire was threatened by Irish Home Rule and evidently had come to the conclusion that this unity was more important than social reform. Hence he resigned. Had he continued in the Cabinet, agreeing to Gladstone's program, he might well have become the next leader of the party, whereas resignation seemed to indicate the death of his ambition to be Prime Minister.

Preparations for the introduction of the Home Rule measure proceeded after Chamberlain's resignation, the bill being introduced on April 9th. Chamberlain spoke against it with vigor, converting many other Liberals to his views, although they were in part influenced by Bright's letter to Chamberlain opposing Home Rule; however, Bright's idea seemed to have been to encourage abstention rather than negative votes. When the vote was taken on the second reading on June 8, 1886, the Government found itself defeated by a majority of 40; 93 Liberals voted against the bill, 46 being followers of Chamberlain; Hartington and the Whig element counted for the remainder. Defeated, the Government appealed to the country where another defeat awaited it. The Opposition returned 316 Conservatives and 78 dissentient Liberals; the Government secured 276 seats, 85 of which were Nationalists.

Chamberlain had succeeded in defeating Home Rule, but he had also split the Liberal Party; he was to perform a like favor for the Conservatives within two decades. This was the decisive point in his career. From this point to the close of his political life social reform became subordinated to what he considered to be the larger interest of the Empire. Since this was the turning point of his career, it is important to examine in detail his position in this connection.

Having once decided upon his course, Chamberlain threw himself into the campaign to defeat the Home Rule bill with greater vigor. Laying aside the hope of personal advancement and breaking with friends of long standing, he made his profession of faith:

"Since I have been in public affairs I have called myself, I think not altogether without reason, a Radical. But that title has never prevented me from giving great consideration to Imperial interests. I have cared for the honour and the influence and the integrity of the Empire, and it is because I believe these things are now in danger that I have felt myself called upon to make the greatest sacrifice any public man can be called to make."[34]

The honor of Britain was at stake; better to have a country to govern, thought Chamberlain, than to lose it because reform seemed impossible.[35]

The plan for setting up a government in Ireland separate and distinct from the government in London would be disastrous to the interests of the United Kingdom. Moreover, it might "destroy the power and the influence of this mighty Empire which has been built up and left us as a heritage by our forefathers, and which has done so much to promote the civilisation and the freedom of the world."[36] Chamberlain considered a policy of disintegration one of sheer folly in view of the fact that all other nations were attempting to consolidate their empires. He feared that once the policy was adopted it would spread, sapping the power of Great Britain.[37] Imperial supremacy was necessary to preserve the integrity of the Empire.[38]

At that point at which the Irish lost their right of representation at Westminster and the Imperial Parliament lost control of Irish taxation and of the Irish judiciary,[39] the influence of the Imperial Parliament in the affairs of Ireland would be gone. Chamberlain did not regard Irish representation at Westminster as a mere technical objection; to him it represented the symbol of "the effective union of the three kingdoms."[40] He did not mean by his insistence on this point to prohibit the organization of a local legislature in Ireland; he favored such bodies provided they were subordinate to the Imperial Parliament and not equal in authority to it.[41] He considered the maintenance of the supremacy of Westminster as the "essential, cardinal, condition" of any changes in the matter of Ireland.[42]

Chamberlain believed that the future of the dream of Imperial federation would be considerably darkened should Ireland dissolve the union existing between it and the other two kingdoms, for, as he wrote to a fellow member of Parliament:

"The hope—it may be only a distant one, but it has infinite attractions—of drawing more closely together the great dependencies of the British Crown and welding them into a mighty and harmonious Empire rests on the determination to resist in their inception all separatist tendencies, and to maintain one central Parliament for the protection of the common interests of all who claim their part in the Imperial organization."[43]

Another reason for maintaining the supremacy of the Imperial Parliament was that only through some such agency could "the property and the lives of all the subjects of the Crown" be protected.[44] Formerly he had been concerned lest the landlords secure too great an advantage; now property became unsafe in the hands of the Irish, who would surely confiscate it.

In Chamberlain's estimation, the right of Ireland to govern itself was conditional and could be granted only if no harm befell the Empire as a result.[45] Ireland was so situated, however, that its independence would become a menace to the peace and security of the neighboring island. Had Ireland been a thousand miles away Chamberlain conceived that the situation would have been drastically different, but, being so near, the strategic interests of Britain demanded that the interests of the smaller country be sacrificed to it.[46] The people of Ireland had long looked upon the English as their natural enemies; once independent, Ireland would embarrass Great Britain in its defense plans—either by condemning British foreign policy[47] or, more seriously, by being conquered by some hostile power and used as a base of operations against England and Scotland.[48]

Chamberlain was of the opinion that the rights of Irish minorities would be threatened if Ireland was allowed to govern itself. The two million Protestants in Ulster would be at the mercy of the majority of Catholic Irishmen. In this connection Chamberlain made some rather invidious comparisons between the two sections, saying that the people of southern Ireland were agitators who cared for no law human or divine, that they were discontented humans who failed in all the qualities that made for success—that, on the other hand, Ulstermen were of a dominant race which had displayed qualities which made its intellectual and commercial ascendancy assured.[49] Less than five years before Chamberlain had praised the qualities of the main body of Irishmen, saying that the only obstacle in their way was the evil system under which they were forced to exist.[50] The Ulstermen, racially, religiously, and sympathetically akin to the English, feared the results of separation; racial pride demanded that they be protected.[51] Ulster ought not to be forced to endure the ignominy of supporting a Catholic church endowed by the state.[52]

Chamberlain vacillated in his attitude toward the question of whether Ireland was or was not a nation. In 1884 he seemed convinced that it was not, particularly if that implied a separate people. Rather than yield to the aspirations of nationality he declared, "I would govern Ireland by force to the end of the chapter."[53] However, in 1886 he was arguing that Ireland was composed of two nations, saying, "it [Ireland] consists of two nations—that it is a nation which comprises two races and two religions."[54] Two years later he declared he would never recognize political nationality in Ireland, although he said he did not want to confuse this with sentimental nationality, which he did not define.[55] Perhaps he meant that he was perfectly content that the Irish should have national sentiments provided they did not result in demands for separation, which may have been, to him, a synonym for "political nationality." He would not grant nationality status to the Irish, for, having granted that much, he would be forced to grant them control over their revenues, military affairs, legislation, and, in short, all those matters which are attributes of statehood.[56] The following year Chamberlain spoke of the four nationalities which comprised the United Kingdom, denying to any of them the right to be called a nation, but claiming that aggregated together they became one nation.[57] He also stated that Ireland had no historic claims to nationhood until the time of the English conquest[58]—therefore they had no claim whatsoever.

One conclusion that stands out from this rather confusing evidence is the fact that Chamberlain had no fixed idea of what a nation was, or, if he had one, he succeeded in disguising it extremely well. In one breath he denied nationality to Ireland; in the next he said that Ireland was one of four nationalities comprising the British nation. Sometimes he said it was a nation composed of two races and two religions. However, he seemed to be endeavoring to say that so long as nationhood, nationality, or nationalism did not involve separation he would recognize it, but at the moment separation became involved he was forced to deny its existence. He seemed to have thought that claims to nationhood were dependent on historic claims of long standing to which Ireland had no rights. The history of the rise of nationalism in the West, however, seems to indicate that this is not necessary. The general conclusion is that peoples become conscious of their nationhood or nationalism as the result of pressure from without; the sentiment is probably lying dormant, until aroused by pressure. China felt no sentiment of nationality until the Western Powers and Japan began their interference. Egyptian nationalism and the nationalism of the other so-called backward peoples developed only after the impact of Western imperialism had been felt. In Europe itself nationalism was a response to outside pressure to a certain extent.[59] So it may well have been that Irish nationalism developed because of the feeling of unity resulting from the consciousness of British oppression.

During the course of the Home Rule struggle the proponents of the measure defended it on the ground that it placed Ireland in a position similar to Canada: a self-governing colony. Chamberlain, however, objected to the measure because it did just that—for Canada was a part of the Empire only so long as she desired to be, the connection being terminable at any time when the Canadians had a desire to do so as "no one would think of employing force in order to tie any reluctant self-governing colony in continued bonds to this country."[60] Canada was only nominally a part of Britain and the latter would exercise no control over it if such control were unpleasant to Canada. Chamberlain was of the opinion that Canada and Australia might break away from Britain in time of war;[61] the ties holding Canada and Australia to the mother country were ties of sentiment only. As far as he was concerned, Canada was practically an independent nation having the right "whenever her interests demand it, to deal with everything in which she is concerned according to her own views and without reference to the views of the mother country—this although the subject under consideration may be one of those which has been withdrawn from her cognizance by the constitution under which she lives."[62]

Whereas the proponents of Home Rule desired to see Ireland a self-governing colony similar to Canada, Chamberlain thought that the proper solution of the Irish question was to give Ireland a status in the United Kingdom similar to the status of a province under the Canadian constitution.[63] Under such an arrangement the subjects acted upon by the Irish legislature would be delegated rather than surrendered and would be subject to revision under certain conditions. The analogy of the Canadian Constitution also provided for separate treatment of provinces differing in race and religion from the others, which fitted the condition of Ireland exactly.[64]

One of Chamberlain's objections to the Home Rule Bill—interesting to note in the light of future events—was that he feared that once given control over their own affairs, the Irish would set up protective duties against British industries.[65] Clearly, Chamberlain was still a free trader. While turning toward imperialism he had not yet seen that a system of protection is a natural corollary to a policy of imperialism.[66]

During the campaign of 1885 Chamberlain had been unrelenting in his attacks on the Tories. He had taunted them as constituting a reactionary party held together by a "Beer and Bible Alliance" and seeking only selfish privilege and power. On one occasion he had even spoken of the impossibility of associating with Tories as a party.[67] The Home Rule Bill and his desire to preserve the union, however, forced him to change his ideas rather drastically. In June of 1887 he was declaring that the Tory Party would solve all the urgent and pressing problems of the day.[68] The next year he was saying that the old Toryism had died out and no representative of the old way of thinking had power in the new Conservative Ministry.[69] Salisbury was Prime Minister at the time; his Cabinet was composed of men the majority of whom had been in his previous Cabinet. Two years before, Chamberlain had been threatening Salisbury, whom he had singled out as the representative of the reactionary class. Had he forgotten so soon? That is hardly to be expected. His one great passion was to preserve the unity of the Empire and this could be done with greater ease by working with the Tories, who agreed with him in this connection. The preservation of the union had become more important than social reform, although in his speeches he attempted to hide this fact by saying that the Conservatives were "anxious . . . to promote all reasonable and safe reforms."[70] Either he or the Tories had changed measurably in the previous two years. A peaceful conversion of reactionaries *en masse* is decidedly a *rare occurrence;* Chamberlain, whether he knew it or not, having decided that the unity of the Empire was the *summum bonum,* necessarily had to modify his other views to make them conform to the new pattern of his life. Formerly he had attacked the House of Lords; now he was its defender, the climax being reached when he praised that body in 1893 as the real representative of the people because it threw out Gladstone's second Home Rule Bill after approval by the House of Commons.[71]

As was seen in Chapter II, the roots of Chamberlain's imperialism were apparent in the earlier years, although his chief concern was with the Radical program of domestic reform. But with the casting of the die in 1885 the Empire assumed larger and larger proportions in his thinking, to the exclusion of his former program. The question arises as to whether or not he changed his views. It is apparent that he had decided as far back as 1874 that separation was not to be tolerated; from that it is easy to conclude that his views on Ireland remained consistently the same. That may be true but one must remember that in those days Chamberlain was much more concerned with the program of social reform then dominating his life.

When the dormant idea became fully awake it assumed a more powerful influence in Chamberlain's life than had his desire for reform. In 1885 there was a clash of ideas. Radicalism came off second best, imperialism being triumphant. One might say that Chamberlain was an imperialist from the beginning, but perhaps it is better to say that although the seeds of imperialism were present, they were not cultivated until the introduction of Home Rule; then they grew so luxuriantly that they virtually crowded out the earlier plant-ideas.

Before the Irish struggles Chamberlain appeared to have formulated no definite ideas about Imperial policy. During the course of the Home Rule fight, however, circumstances forced him to consider certain problems heretofore neglected. One of the reasons for his desire to retain Ireland, it developed, was that strategic considerations made that island a vital part of England's defense system. However, the proponents of Home Rule only envisioned that Ireland should become a self-governing colony similar to Canada; as far as the Empire was concerned it was still to be British territory. Admitting that foreign powers might be able to embarrass Great Britain by using Ireland as a base of operations, it is doubtful that such a step would be attempted so long as the British flag still waved over Ireland. Even had the Home Rule Bill gone farther and granted complete independence to Ireland, the threat to British defensive strategy might have been lessened by some agreement allowing Great Britain the right to maintain military and naval bases in Ireland just as the United States maintains a naval base at Guantanamo Bay, Cuba.

It was Chamberlain's opinion that Ireland must be bound closer to England than by mere sentimental ties if Imperial federation was ever to succeed. At a time when the Empire was trying to draw itself together it seemed unwise to him to loosen the ties binding Ireland. One wonders whether Ireland might not have been drawn closer to the Empire if the ties binding them together were sentimental only. Had that been the case when Imperial federation was attempted, Ireland would have been the equal of Canada and other self-governing colonies and it would have been able to have a voice in Imperial affairs; however, as a part of the United Kingdom, its voice in such affairs was overborne by the more dominant partner.

Chamberlain's definition of the position of the self-governing colonies in the Empire is quite interesting. He practically gave them the status of independent states when he said that the tie could be terminated at the slightest provocation and that they might even legislate on affairs expressly defined as being beyond their powers in the enabling acts. It was not until the passage of the Statute of Westminster in 1931 that the Dominions actually and legally possessed the status that Chamberlain seemed willing to confer in 1887.

Chamberlain's stand on the Irish question not only signalled the awakening of an Imperialist, it also involved the breakup of the Liberal Party. After the split of 1886 the "party of progress" never regained its old vitality. Out of office for two decades, with the exception of the brief interval from 1892 to 1894, its return to power in 1906 was the signal for a renewal of reform legislation, which was interrupted by the First World War. After that war the Labor Party usurped the place of the Liberals as the "party of progress."

Within the short space of two years, Chamberlain had taken a position from which his later imperialism may be traced. This later imperialism grew naturally from the ideas that he expressed during the Irish struggle; that struggle had embittered him and made him oppose certain domestic policies. His Imperial policy thus came to absorb the political energy which he had once expended in behalf of domestic reform. Having broken with the Liberals, he tended to gravitate toward the Conservative Party which, besides opposing Home Rule, had always been the party of imperialism. Within the next fifteen years Chamberlain, working with the Conservatives, developed his Imperial policy. But in 1903 his imperialism, issuing in protection, was also to divide the Conservatives.

REFERENCES

[1]Boyd, *op. cit.*, I, 28.
[2]Garvin, *op. cit.*, I, 273.
[3]*Ibid.*, 118.
[4]*Ibid.*, 318–9.
[5]*Ibid.*, 329.
[6]Lucy, *op. cit.*, 27; Joseph Chamberlain, *Home Rule and the Irish Question* (London, 1887), 10.
[7]Garvin, *op cit.*, 343.
[8]Harold J. Laski, *Democracy in Crisis* (Chapel Hill, 1933), 266.
[9]Garvin, *op. cit.*, 344.
[10]John Stuart Mill, *England and Ireland* (London, 1868).
[11]Boyd, *op. cit.*, 238–9.
[12]J. L. Hammond, *Gladstone and the Irish Nation* (London, 1938), 352.
[13]Garvin, *op. cit.*, 345.
[14]Hammond, *op. cit.*, 497.
[15]See his speeches, *Home Rule and the Irish Question* (London, 1887).
[16]*The Times*, December 17, 1888.
[17]Mill , *op. cit.*, 10-44.
[18]Cf. Garvin, *op. cit.*, 358-68; Hammond, *op. cit.*, 348 ff.
[19]Lucy, *op. cit.*, 68.
[20]*Ibid.*, 96.
[21]Speech quoted in *The Times*, June 4, 1885.
[22]Speech quoted *ibid.*, June 18, 1885.
[23]Lucy, *op. cit.*, 185.
[24]Garvin, *op. cit.*, 145.
[25]*Ibid.*, 172.
[26]Stephen Gwynn and G. M. Tuckwell, *The Life of the Right Hon. Sir Charles W. Dilke* (New York, 1917), II, 205.
[27]Garvin, *op. cit.*, I, 529.
[28]*Ibid.*, II, 177.
[29]*Ibid.*, 188.
[30]*Ibid.*, 192.
[31]John M. Robertson, *Chamberlain, A Study* (London, 1905), 32.
[32]Gardiner, *op. cit.*, I, 586.
[33]*Ibid.*, II, 19.
[34]*Hansard*, Third Series, v. 304, p. 1183.
[35]Joseph Chamberlain, *Speeches on the Irish Question* (London, 1890), 46.
[36]Boyd, *op. cit.*, I, 255.
[37]*Irish Speeches*, op. cit., 137.

38*The Times*, January 31, 1887.

39*Hansard*, Third Series, v. 304, pp. 1190-1.

40Quoted in *The Times*, May 13, 1886; *Home Rule Speeches*, 104, carries similar statement.

41*Ibid.*, 107.

42Boyd, *op. cit.*, 293.

43Quoted in *The Times*, May 8, 1886.

44Quoted, *ibid.*, June 25, 1886.

45*Ibid.*, March 29, 1887.

46*Hansard*, Fourth Series, v. 8, p. 1721.

47*Ibid.*, v. 12, p. 1611.

48*Ibid.*, v. 8, p. 1727.

49Boyd, *op. cit.*, 287-88.

50Lucy, *op. cit.*, 22.

51Boyd,*op. cit.*, 281.

52*Irish Speeches, op. cit.*, 167.

53Sir Charles Petrie, *The Chamberlain Tradition* (London, 1938), 72.

54*Hansard*, Third Series, v. 304, p. 1200.

55Boyd, *op. cit.*, 310-11.

56*Irish Speeches, op. cit.*, 217-18.

57*Ibid.*, 33.

58*Ibid.*, 172.

59Cf. Bernard Joseph, *Nationalism* (London, 1929). Also seminar notes on Nationalism under Professor Rupert Emerson at Harvard University.

60Boyd, *op. cit.*, 244.

61*Ibid.*, 278.

62Quoted in *The Times*, October 26, 1887.

63*Ibid.*, April 25, 1887.

64*Ibid.*, January 7, 1887.

65*Irish Speeches, op. cit.*, 171.

66Cf. J. A. Hobson, *Imperialism, A Study* (London, 1905), p. 60.

67Lucy, *op. cit.*, 181.

68*The Times*, June 15, 1887.

69Boyd, *op. cit.*, 299.

70*Ibid.*, 300.

71*The Times*, September 10, 1893.

The Development of Imperialism

Having "killed the bill," Chamberlain departed for a tour in the lands east of the Mediterranean. While in Turkey he had an interview with the Sultan concerning the development of Turkish railways. He advised the Sultan that financiers were not interested in strategic railroads; if Turkey wanted capital to develop railroads it must consent to build commercial lines first. Chamberlain drew up a scheme for the Sultan which linked the proposed Turkish lines with some other proposed lines for China. A few months previously, Chamberlain had drawn up a memorandum for Lord Rosebery, the President of the Board of Trade in Gladstone's Cabinet of 1886. Based on information gleaned while Chamberlain had held that post, it urged that the Government give approval to loans for railway construction in China.[1] Lord Rosebery ignored this advice. The plan for Turkish railroads was not revived until the Germans began the Berlin-to-Bagdad railway.

Returning to England he hoped for a possible reunion of the factions of the Liberal Party. The Round Table Conference, called for the purpose of formulating an agreement on policy in January and February of 1887, failed to accomplish the desired end—as did the conversation of Chamberlain and Gladstone at Dollis Hill soon afterward. Refusing to yield in his unbending opposition to Home Rule, Chamberlain remained stranged from the Liberals although he refused to identify himself with the Conservatives and did not cross the floor of Parliament to sit with them. While he did not work with the Conservatives, however, he supported their policies in a large measure. His occasional failure to extend support irritated the Conservative leadership; it desired to see him out of Parliament for a time. Chamberlain himself was rather desirous of taking an extended vacation as the struggle over Ireland had left him somewhat embittered. The Conservatives knew of his inclinations. W. H. Smith, the leader of the House, thought that his absence would relieve an embarrassing situation and, after receiving Chamberlain's assent, he suggested to Prime Minister Salisbury that Chamberlain be appointed to head the British delegation going to Washington to settle the fishing dispute—then at an acute stage—between Canadian and New England fishermen.[2]

Disputes over fishing rights had characterized Anglo-American relations ever since the British recognized the independence of the Thirteen Colonies. After the Revolutionary War, the United States gained the right to continue to fish in the off-shore waters of the British North American Colonies, but this privilege was revoked after the War of 1812. Then followed a period without much regulation, terminated by a reciprocal agreement in 1854, which was abrogated by the United States in the sixties only to be renewed by a similar treaty in 1871. The latter treaty, however, expired in 1885; as a result, Canada lost the right to import fish freely into the American market while the American fishing boats lost the right to use Canadian waters save in emergencies. Although legally the Gloucestermen had no right to fish in Canadian waters the practice continued, much to the irritation of the Canadians who could no longer ship fish to the American market without paying an excessive duty. In retaliation the Canadian government began to detain American fishing vessels, charging them with illegal trespass. While the British Government was immersed in the Home Rule squabble, the situation on this side of the Atlantic grew worse.

In August of 1887 the Cleveland Administration suggested to Great Britain that a joint Commission be appointed to settle the differences. Of this Commission Chamberlain became the British chief. His years as President of the Board of Trade had acquainted him with maritime matters of all sorts; he was also well-versed in Canadian affairs as a result of his recent study of its constitution in connection with his Irish stand. Since the sympathies of the American Irish were for Home Rule, it may have been unwise to appoint him head of the Commission, but all the leaders in the Unionist ranks had spoken against Home Rule. Salisbury would have had to choose from the ranks of the Gladstonians if he had wanted to appoint an advocate of Home Rule.

The Joint Commission met in Washington on November 21, 1887, and drew up a treaty which was signed on February 15, 1888. This treaty never became law, being rejected by the U. S. Senate about six months later, but the essential agreement of the two countries was assured since the Commission had also signed a Protocol providing a *modus vivendi* until the treaty was signed. This Protocol was renewed from year to year until a definitive treaty was signed in 1912.[3]

When the Commission recessed, Chamberlain paid a visit to Canada. At the Board of Trade dinner given for him in Toronto on December 30, 1887, he spoke with considerable pride about the British race and the British Empire, a trait which was to characterize his future political life. He was impressed with an idea:

"That idea is the greatness and importance of the destiny which is reserved for the Anglo-Saxon race—for that proud, persistent, self-asserting, and resolute stock, that no change of climate or condition can alter, and which is infallibly destined to be the predominant force in the future history and civilisation of the world."[4]

He linked pride of race with patriotism but he made it plain that that patriotism ought to extend beyond the bounds of England to include the whole Empire and even the United States; he used the term "Greater Britain" in the same sense in which Dilke had used it almost twenty years earlier.[5] The English were engaged in a civilizing mission, spreading "English love of liberty and law" throughout the world. Because this was so there could be no distinction between Englishmen living at home and Englishmen living in their respective colonies, or even between Englishmen and Americans. To the colonists he said, "You cannot if you would break the invisible bonds which bind us together."[6] He assured them that if they wished to continue as an integral part of the Empire their interests would be maintained by the influence and power which the Empire had at its command.[7] He pointed out that the Canadian Federation might serve as a model for the future federation of the Empire.[8]

Returning to England in the spring to receive the praise of the Queen and the Prime Minister, Chamberlain aligned himself more closely with the Conservatives although he did not sit with them in Parliament, preferring to sit with the Liberals, a fact probably irritating to the latter. While still expressing interest in domestic affairs, he turned more and more to Imperial affairs, the activities of the self-governing colonies, and the possibilities of Empire federation. From this time on he was an emphatic Imperialist. Speaking to the London Chamber of Commerce on May 14, 1888, he declared his faith not only in the preservation of the Empire, but in its free extension in Africa because that was necessary as a means of furthering "necessary work of colonisation and civilisation" and in order to "justify our position as a nation."[9]

In the autumn of 1889 Chamberlain made an extended tour of

Egypt, interviewing not only the British officials (from Sir Evelyn Baring down) but also the Egyptian authorities. His findings convinced him that Great Britain must remain in Egypt.[10] Garvin is of the opinion that the trip crystallized Chamberlain's thinking and made him an Imperialist.[11] That the trip resulted in a crystallization of his thought there can be no doubt, but the evidence seems to indicate that the Irish question made him an Imperialist. Returning to Birmingham, Chamberlain spoke of his impressions of Egypt and Egyptian affairs. In recounting the history of England's occupation of Egypt, he said that it was necessary to protect the interests of the creditors of Egypt and all those "who had honestly invested capital in industrial enterprises in that country."[12] As has been noted in Chapter II, Chamberlain had been an advocate of intervention in Egypt in 1880, but then he had based his argument on the plight of the fellaheen; intervention ought to be for the purpose of giving the right of self-determination to the disinherited masses. Then he was seeking means to separate the interests of the bondholders from the other causes for intervention. How his views changed within ten years!

In listing the advantages that had accrued to Egypt because of British intervention, Chamberlain mentioned the fact that the finances of the country had been restored, that a surplus existed, that programs of public works and national education were under way, that courts of justice had replaced a corrupt judicial system, that the *corvee* and conscription were gradually being reduced, that an irrigation system provided water to rich and poor alike.[13] He made no mention of any progress in local self-government or of the extension of liberties to the fellaheen. Formerly he had been of the opinion that England had no right to force an efficient system upon the Egyptians if they preferred the old corrupt one; in 1890 he was mainly interested in the fruits of an efficient administration. The improvement of conditions in Egypt he ascribed solely to the influence of the British.[14] But although much had been done, so much remained yet to be accomplished that to retire from Egypt would be unworthy of Britain.[15]

Fearing that the return of Gladstone would mean the evacuation of Egypt, Chamberlain warned the electorate that such a step would mean the undoing of all the good work done. Moreover, he added that evacuation would mean that some other European nation would step in and reap the advantages thrown away by Great Britain.[16] International politics then being what they were, Chamberlain's contention was probably right, a fact which was certainly a strong argu-

ment for remaining. If Egypt was to be the victim of foreign interference in any event it was better that England should remain rather
than that some other nation should come in to take control.

When the Gladstone Government took office in August, 1892,
Lord Rosebery, the Liberal Imperialist, was Foreign Secretary. This
situation insured the continuation of the British occupation of Egypt,
Rosebery having accepted office with that understanding. The circumstances cheered Chamberlain, who had feared evacuation as a
result of the change of government.[17] He had rejoiced that Britain
would continue to secure Egypt "against foreign invasion and against
domestic anarchy and disorder"; that this had been done by less than
one hundred and fifty Englishmen was in his estimation "one of the
most creditable incidents in British history."[18]

In 1888 Chamberlain began to emphasize the connection between
trade and Empire. The reason for this was probably the decline in
British trade, then becoming apparent, together with the rise of Germany as a commercial competitor. Chamberlain desired to strengthen
the bonds which held the colonies to the mother country, for, in his
opinion, trade followed the flag.[19] Sentiment, he thought, played a
great part in commercial transactions; Englishmen preferred to deal
with fellow Englishmen. If the Empire were drawn closer together,
inter-Empire trade would naturally increase.[20] Believing that trade
followed the flag, Chamberlain was convinced that to reduce the size
of the Empire would perforce reduce British trade; and any considerable reduction in the size of the Empire would result in the starvation
of a great proportion of the inhabitants of the United Kingdom.[21]
While the burdens of the Empire might be tremendous, preservation
and extension was an economic necessity.[22] These considerations led
Chamberlain to advocate formation of a united system of Empire defense and a commercial union—a plan of Empire federation. However,
he had doubts regarding the possibility of commercial union because
he did not think the colonies would abandon their tariffs unless Britain
abandoned free trade and he did not believe that Britain ought to
sacrifice this principle to the interests of the colonies.[23] Hence, he
thought the efforts for Empire federation ought to be based on plans
for Empire defense designed to unite "the kindred races and . . .
nations that own our rule."[24]

Chamberlain was desirous of perfecting plans for a centralized
defense system in order to draw the Empire together into an integrated
unit. He was convinced that the day of small nations was passed and

that the future history of the world would be determined by the great Empire states.[25] The British people had created a vast Empire which could dominate world affairs provided it always acted as a unit. Since, however, the self-governing colonies were practically independent states,[26] Britain could not depend on Canada and Australia coming to her aid in time of war.[27] By some means the Empire must be drawn closer together. A plan of mutual defense seemed to Chamberlain to offer the best opportunity to accomplish this end.[28]

In preaching his gospel of the expansion of the Empire, Chamberlain made an appeal to the working classes. He declared that hope of continuous employment rested on the extension of the Empire since other nations were closing their borders to British trade; without the maintenance of the Empire and extension of it at every opportunity the future of Britain's working classes would not be bright.[29] It had not been many years since he had argued that the working classes had no interest in a policy of universal dominion and aggressive expansion;[30] then he had based his plea upon the belief that expansion led naturally to conscription, which was abhorrent to the laborers.

Early in 1891 Chamberlain, in speaking to a few African chiefs visiting the Birmingham Small Arms Company, said that in previous years expansion of the Empire had taken place under circumstances of "great injustice, oppression, and corruption."[31] He was of the opinion, however, that this was not a necessary concomitant of expansion and that it would not occur in the future expansion of the British Empire.

In the early nineties, the European Powers provided for the partition of Africa in a series of agreements. During this time there was much talk about "the scramble for Africa." Chamberlain believed that the majority of the English people thought that Britain was in duty bound to take her part in spreading the values of European civilization over the dark continent. This he thought was "justified by the spirit of the past, justified by the spirit of adventure and enterprise which has rendered us, of all nations, peculiarly fitted to carry out the work of colonization."[32] He declared on March 20, 1893: "I believe in the expansion of the Empire . . . [I am] not at all troubled by accusations of Jingoism."[33] He thought that history demonstrated that it was "the manifest destiny of this country to be a great colonizing and civilizing Power."[34] He was convinced that to lay down a principle to the effect that no further expansion would be attempted would be to strike at "the root cause of our great prosperity and position."[35] Such a principle would also imperil the position of Britain as one of the great European Powers since that would be tantamount to shirking its responsibility to civilization.[36] If some raised objections to his policy on the ground that expansion was costly, Chamberlain replied that "duty and honor" could not be measured in monetary terms.[37]

One of the reasons Chamberlain offered for continued British expansion in Africa was that expansion would cut down the slave trade. Pointing out that slaves were then used for portage, he argued that if Britain took control of an area railroads would be built and the need for slaves ended.[38] Moreover, he pointed out, if Britain neglected to take its share of Africa the other European Powers would step in and claim that which Britain had ignored. He did not think that Britain could afford to be worsted by her rivals.[39] With all his desire for expansion, Chamberlain was convinced that the Empire must do something more than expand. "It is not," he said, "enough to occupy certain great spaces of the earth's surface unless you can make the best of them, unless you are willing to develop them. We are landlords of a great estate; it is the duty of the landlord to develop his estate."[40]

From the time of the defeat of the Home Rule Bill until his selection as Colonial Secretary in 1895, Chamberlain's interest in Imperial affairs increased. It was in this period that his belief in the superiority of the British race had taken definite root and that he had expressed confidence that the Anglo-Saxon race would dominate the future. These attitudes were to continue in his later years as Colonial Secretary.

It is during this period that the question of trade first entered into Chamberlain's ideas as to Imperial policy. He did not as yet advocate the reversal of the policy of free trade, as he was to do later in his career, but the tariff policies of other countries convinced him that Britain must extend its trade with the Empire and add to the Empire in order to extend trade further, for he believed that trade followed the flag. The truth of the matter was that trade followed the price list, not the flag. Britain's trade was declining because the other nations sold similar goods for less. That trade did not follow the flag the statistics demonstrated; Britain then carried on more commerce with foreign states than within the Empire.[41] This was true despite the fact that since 1880 the Empire had grown by leaps and bounds.

During the period 1880-1884, as has been noted, Chamberlain was primarily interested in domestic politics and quite definitely opposed to a policy of Imperial expansion. However, the Irish question turned his attention away from domestic reform and toward Imperial politics, which naturally led him to support the Conservative Party. But his past actions made the change from the Liberal Party to the Conservative a difficult one. He was torn between a desire to remain within the ranks of the Liberals and convert them to his way of thinking and a desire to support the Conservatives who had made his fight against Home Rule successful. His vacillation from one side to the other on the various votes taken in Parliament made his presence obnoxious to both groups. His selection for the mission sent to America seemed to have been a happy solution to the problem. Upon his return, however, his position appeared to have changed slightly. No longer did he vacillate from the Liberals to the Conservatives; he had become an out-and-out Tory, and so he remained until he resigned from the Cabinet over his tariff reform measures. His interest in the Empire was extended considerably by his visit to the United States and Canada. This interest increased when he visited Egypt in 1889; upon his return he was a full-fledged Imperialist, as Garvin has noted.

In this period one sees the adumbration of those ideas which were to be the moving force of his career in the years following his acceptance of the Colonial Office. Whereas in the earlier period he had expressed himself in opposition to a policy of expansion and aggression, in this period expansion became for him the chief reason for prosperity of Britain; if before he had thought the masses had no interest in the expansion of the Empire, now expansion was the *sine qua non* of the future well-being of the working classes. During this period he began to express an interest in the possibilities of Empire federation either through a defense league or a commercial union, although he did not develop any scheme to organize either. In only one respect was his policy in this period similar to that of the earlier period; he continued in his desire that Britain should circumvent and thwart the actions of other Powers in their effort to expand.

REFERENCES

[1]Garvin, *op. cit.*, II, 449-50.
[2]*Ibid.*, 325.
[3]*Ibid.*, 328-30.
[4]Joseph Chamberlain, *Foreign and Colonial Speeches* (London, 1897), 6.
[5]Cf. C. W. Dilke, *Greater Britain* (London, 1869).
[6]*For. & Col. Speeches, op. cit.*, 7.
[7]*Ibid.*, 12.
[8]*Ibid.*, 13.
[9]*Ibid.*, 200.
[10]Garvin, *op. cit.*, 454.
[11]*Ibid.*, 447.
[12]*For. & Col. Speeches, op. cit.*, 35.

13*Ibid.*, 39-41.
14*Ibid.*, 42.
15*Ibid.*
16*The Times,* October 22, 1891.
17*Hansard,* Fourth Series, v. 10, p. 277.
18*Ibid.*, 279.
19Boyd, *op. cit.*, I, 323; *The Times,* January 26, 1889.
20Boyd, *op. cit.*, 324.
21*For. & Col. Speeches, op. cit.*, 202.
22*Ibid.*, 203.
23Boyd, *op. cit.*, 324.
24Quoted in *The Times,* January 26, 1889.
25*Irish Speeches, op. cit.*, 175.
26*Ibid.*, 183.
27*Hansard,* Fourth Series, v. 8, p. 1720.
28*The Times,* January 26 and 29, 1889.
29*Ibid.*, February 6, 1893; September 28, 1894.
30Boyd, *op. cit.*, 134.
31Quoted in *The Times,* July 23, 1891.
32Boyd, *op. cit.*, 344.
33*Ibid.*, 347.
34*Hansard,* Fourth Series, v. 25, p. 253.
35*Ibid.*, p. 254.
36*Ibid.*, v. 10, p. 284.
37Boyd, *op. cit.*, 348.
38*Ibid.*, 354.
39*Hansard,* Fourth Series, v. 25, p. 255.
40Quoted in *The Times,* April 1, 1895.
41Cf. V. Berard, *British Imperialism and Colonial Policy* (New York, 1906), 193; also Hobson, *op. cit.*, 301.

The Imperialist in Action

When Parliament assembled in 1895 it was apparent that the Rosebery Government could not survive. It was only a question of time before the Conservatives would assume office. What part would Chamberlain play in the formation of the new Ministry? Lord Randolph Churchill had referred to the Liberal Unionists as the "crutch" of the Conservative Party; without the former the latter would have had only a weak Government. It seemed natural that Chamberlain should play an active part in the forthcoming developments. He had, after all, given the Conservatives his active support almost continuously since 1887. However, there were many among them who disliked Chamberlain and his influence—they remembered the campaign of 1885. They made their opposition felt through the pages of the Conservative journals. Never at ease under fire, Chamberlain became angry at the attacks.

In March of 1895 he threatened to break with the Tories and retire from politics. Speaker Peel was on the point of resigning; the Liberal Unionists anticipated that his seat would be theirs without the contest which the Conservatives threatened. Chamberlain felt that by contesting the seat the Conservatives were indicating their disapproval of his actions and policies; incensed at this, he had almost resolved to teach "the old stupid party" one last lesson and retire. Salisbury, however, succeeded in convincing him that his services were appreciated. The Conservatives decided not to contest the seat and Chamberlain remained their ally.

Not long after this interlude the Rosebery Cabinet fell when on June 21, 1896, Parliament censured the Secretary of War for not having a sufficient supply of cordite on hand, and Salisbury went in as Prime Minister. On June 23, Salisbury summoned the prospective leaders of his Cabinet to determine which offices they were to have. Present were Salisbury, the Duke of Devonshire, A. J. Balfour, and Joseph Chamberlain. Devonshire asked for the Lord Presidency of the Council; he did not desire the Foreign Office because of its strenuous duties. Salisbury next offered Chamberlain any office he wished, including the Chancellorship of the Exchequer. Chamberlain indicated his preference for the Colonies although he was willing to be Secretary of State for War if the others so desired. (It will be recalled that he had refused the Admiralty eight years previously on the ground that one of his views ought not to head a great spending department. Did his action in 1895 indicate that he no longer thought of himself as a Radical?) Having settled upon Chamberlain as Colonial Secretary, Balfour assumed, in addition to his duties as Leader of the House of Commons, the office of First Lord of the Treasury.[1]

Chamberlain's choice of the Colonial Office occasioned considerable surprise as the post was considered to be one of comparative unimportance. It is hardly likely that Chamberlain had any presentiment at this time that the protracted war he was to wage against the Boers would make the Colonial Office one of the strongest in the Cabinet. However, any position he might have selected, would naturally have become one of primary consequence, for he entered the Cabinet virtually as co-head; indeed, his influence was superior to that of Salisbury. Chamberlain's declared purpose on entering his new office was to bring about a closer federation of the Empire, a field of endeavor certainly replete with possibilities. As Colonial Secretary, Chamberlain had under his personal supervision the activities of the eleven self-governing colonies.

For some years he had been interested in colonial affairs; this interest had been heightened through his study of the Canadian constitution during the fight over Home Rule, his stay in America, and his travels in Egypt. He had also studied *The Expansion of England* by Professor Seeley and the two well-known works of his friend, Charles Dilke: *Greater Britain* and *The Problems of Greater Britain*. Taking up his duties, Chamberlain augmented his knowledge of colonial affairs by making himself available to all overseas visitors who might have valuable intelligence to impart. He also made extensive use of his permanent staff, one of his favorite officials being Lord Lugard; he also relied on Miss Flora Shaw—later Lady Lugard—for much information on colonial questions.[2]

Chamberlain had not been in office long, when he was able to share in a decision which resulted in the consummation of his earlier desire to retake Khartoum. On March 1, 1896, an Italian force had met disaster at the hands of the Ethiopians at Adowa. Following this blow to white supremacy in Africa, the dervishes threatened an Italian garrison at Kassala. The Italian Government then requested the British to divert the attention of the natives by sending an expedition up the Nile. Chamberlain favored such a move, but he advised the Prime Minister that Kitchener should be instructed to proceed with extreme caution.[3] That these instructions were followed was evidenced by the fact that Kitchener did not reach Khartoum until September, 1898.

In defending his stand before Parliament on March 20, 1896, Chamberlain persisted in his contention that Britain had intervened only temporarily in Egypt. The new expedition, in his opinion, had merely demonstrated that the organization of a self-supporting Egypt was a more difficult task than had been anticipated a decade before.[4] However, some of his remarks at the conclusion of his address seemed to indicate that he had no intention of ever advocating British withdrawal from Egypt. For in discussing the railroad which Kitchener was to build in the Sudan as he advanced, Chamberlain declared:

"The making of the railway may, I think, be assumed to be a pledge that where we go we shall remain. We have no idea of handing back to barbarism such territory—be it more or less—as we may recover for civilisation."[5]

Continuing his remarks on the situation in the Sudan, Chamberlain declared that the advance would be limited by the ability of the army to keep its lines of communication open and by the "nature and the extent of the resistance."[6] The primary purpose of sending troops was to prevent any considerable rising on the part of those natives encouraged by the victory at Adowa. Such a rising, Chamberlain indicated, might destroy the fruits of European civilization that Egypt enjoyed as a result of British occupation. An additional reason for the expedition toward Khartoum was the fact that control of the Nile—the lifeblood of Egypt—was essential to the security of Britain.[7]

The latter motive received stress two years later, when Captain Marchand, commanding a small French force, appeared at Fashoda—an evidence of the French desire for control of the Nile. Then Chamberlain expressed himself as firmly opposed to any concession. British claims to all the regions formerly held by the Egyptians were beyond dispute, in his opinion, and the Government ought not to discuss the principle involved. Possession of the Nile was necessary in order to insure that "the sacrifices we have made" in bringing prosperity to Egypt would not be threatened by the actions of an unfriendly or hostile Power which might assume control if Britain abandoned her claims.[8] Tension relaxed when, in March of 1899, the French agreed to withdraw and to make no claims beyond the watershed of the Congo.[9]

Soon after his entry into office, Chamberlain faced a decision of minor importance regarding slave-trading inland from the Gold Coast. Prempeh, Chief of the Ashantis, had been defeated by Wolseley in 1874 and had been forced to sign a treaty (which he did not observe) promising to cease trafficking in slaves. Chamberlain demanded that Prempeh abolish the slave trade in his domain and that he accept a British protectorate. This ultimatum being ignored, Chamberlain asked the War Office to send an expedition to enforce his demands; the expedition was successful without the necessity of fighting.[10]

It was South Africa which most engrossed Chamberlain's thought and action. Here conditions had changed considerably since the Colonial Secretary had advocated the return of the Transvaal. In 1886 gold in large quantities was discovered in the Witwatersrand, and large numbers of Europeans emigrated there in search of the yellow metal. These Europeans—called Uitlanders by the Boers—were not well received by the pastoral and agricultural inhabitants of the South African Republic, for few of the newcomers had any thought of becoming permanent residents; their main motive was to find quick fortune. The Boers rather reluctantly admitted them, withholding from them the rights of citizenship. In addition, they taxed the European miners rather heavily. The result was that the local government remained in the hands of the Boers, although they became a minority through the heavy immigration of the Uitlanders. Clashes of interest naturally resulted between the two groups. Immigrant agitation for ordinary political privileges seemed spontaneous enough—although it may well have been begun by Wernher Beit, Cecil Rhodes, and those capitalists chiefly interested in gaining control of the government to further their own interests.[11]

Rhodes and the De Beers Company had gained control over large economic enterprises in South Africa, Rhodes using his vast capital to further his dreams of Empire which included, among other ambitions, a railroad to Cairo. In order to extend his road north the more easily, Rhodes had repeatedly requested the Colonial Office to transfer the control of the Bechuanaland Protectorate to his company, asserting this would enable him to construct a railway from Mafeking to Buluwayo within four years. He had made these pleas while the Rosebery Government was yet in office, but had met with refusal; now he repeated his proposal. The native chiefs in Bechuanaland objected to the transfer, but in the end Chamberlain consented to give Rhodes a strip through which the railroad would run; it was an area that bordered on the South African Protectorate.

Meanwhile, the actions of President Kruger were giving the Uitlanders additional cause for complaint. The Boers were trying to establish connections with the seacoast which would not be in the hands of the British, and they succeeded in constructing a road to Delagoa Bay. Then, in order to force traffic over this road, Kruger placed heavy tariffs on goods imported from the Cape over the railroad to Johannesburg. To avoid paying these excessive rates the miners resorted to the use of wagons for transporting the goods within the Transvaal. In retaliation, Kruger closed the fords over the river. The Colonial Secretary, advised by the Law Officers of the Crown that such action was contrary to the Convention of 1884, ordered Kruger to lift the ban on the fords and to impose no discriminatory charges on the importation of goods from the Cape.[12]

Kruger's actions in this connection were only typical of the many irritations troubling the Uitlanders. In order to change the situation, they decided a revolution was necessary. Rhodes and his associates were the chief forces in formulating the plans for the uprising that followed, Rhodes sending his brother to Johannesburg to represent him. The De Beers Company financed the arming of the rebels and smuggled the arms into the Transvaal. The rebellion was to begin in Johannesburg during the last week of December, 1895. Upon its outbreak Dr. Jameson, stationed at Pitsani with a small force of Chartered Company police, was to march to the aid of the Johannesburgers, using as an excuse a letter furnished him by the conspirators asking for aid in the protection of property and the lives of women and children.

There may be some doubt that Chamberlain knew of the part which Jameson was scheduled to play in the Transvaal uprising, but he was quite fully informed of the plans taking shape at Johannesburg.[13] He recorded in his "Memorandum" in the autumn of 1895:

"With the grievances of the Uitlanders to which this state of things was due —I have very little sympathy. It seemed to me . . . that a revolution which should succeed in remedying such a state of things would both receive and deserve a large measure of sympathy. . . . There was general concurrence in the information both from private and official sources that matters could not long remain as they were without some serious trouble."[14]

Knowing that the rising was scheduled to take place on December 26, Robinson, the High Commissioner of South Africa, had written Chamberlain asking for authority to go to Pretoria and mediate the dispute. Robinson wanted authority to call a Constituent Assembly elected by manhood suffrage.[15] The Colonial Secretary concurred in this, thankful that the small force under Jameson at Pitsani could be used to support the action of the High Commissioner.[16]

So things were set by the first week in December for the rebellion which was to take place within a short time. But by the middle of December reports began to come to the Colonial Office that the enthusiasm of the Johannesburgers was waning; that German opposition to England and support of the Boers seemed possible. Sir Robert Meade, an official of the Colonial Office, queried Chamberlain as to whether or not he thought it best to postpone the movement for a time. Chamberlain replied on December 18:

"It seems to me that it [the rebellion] should come *at once* or be postponed for a year or two at least. Can we insure this?

"If not we had better not interfere, for we may bring about the very thing we want to avoid."[17]

Another official of the Colonial Office, Fairfield, was of the opinion that matters had gone too far in Johannesburg to be postponed. He was also of the opinion that the rebellion would have a favorable effect upon mining stocks on the London exchange.[18] Fairfield was in unofficial communication with Rochfort Maguire, who was in the confidence of the Rhodes group, and when the Colonial Office decided that it was best to commence the "flotation" in Johannesburg at once, Rhodes and Beit were so informed.[19]

Everything seemed in readiness for the outbreak on December 26, but in Johannesburg a dispute occurred over the question of the flag to be used. Should it be the British banner or the Transvaal flag? Trivial as this question may now seem, it spelled the end of the revolution. By December 29, Chamberlain was writing to Salisbury that the Transvaal business had "fizzled out."[20] But even though the Johannesburgers wavered there was Jameson with his small force at Pitsani, three miles from the Transvaal, waiting for the signal to "go in." Rumors reached the Colonial Office that Rhodes might order Jameson to march even if there was no disturbance at Johannesburg, whereupon Chamberlain advised Robinson to remind Rhodes that such a step would be in violation of his rights under the charter given his company by the British Government.[21]

The impetuous Jameson, at Pitsani, had learned that the Johannesburgers would remain quiet, but he decided to march in the hope that his example would inspire the more cautious Uitlanders. So he wired to Johannesburg that he would start, and also informed Rhodes to that effect. On December 29 he set out, being joined by about 150 others from Mafeking the next day. The excuse for marching in was provided by the letter which Jameson had secured earlier from Johannesburg. Publication of the letter in *The Times* made Jameson a hero rather than a filibuster. Upon hearing of Jameson's action Chamberlain wired Robinson to dispatch a messenger to recall him; Robinson issued a proclamation denouncing the raid and Rhodes publicly disavowed his support of it. Chamberlain himself wired President Kruger that the Government repudiated the action of the raiders.[22]

But what of Jameson? With fewer than 500 men he could not hope to succeed unless he gained help from the Uitlanders. He found his progress impeded from the beginning by ignorance of the terrain and by the lack of remounts which he had expected to be provided. Moreover, the swiftness and the dispatch with which the Boers assembled to block his way was disconcerting. By January 2, his expedition, too, had "fizzled out," the raiders surrendering on that day.

The following day the German Emperor sent his now famous telegram to Kruger congratulating him on his success in withstanding the invasion. The effect of this telegram was to turn the attention of the British people form the raid itself to a feeling of indignation against Germany, which was accompanied by a new sentiment of respect for Jameson. The telegram, of course, pleased Kruger and his associates since it strengthened their position. Thus, when Robinson arrived in Pretoria to act as a mediator he found Kruger adamant. Refusing to make any concessions to the Uitlanders, Kruger demanded complete independence.[23] For the moment he was the victor; the British were in no position to enforce their demands for reform.

When Parliament met in February, 1896, there was naturally a demand for an inquiry into the raid. The Select Committee, appointed for this purpose, did not make its report until the following year. At that time it condemned Rhodes, who had in the meantime resigned as Prime Minister of the Cape Colony, for his part in the raid; Chamberlain, who had not been implicated by this committee, of which he was a member, signed the report; in defending it before Parliament he attempted to minimize the culpability of the "Colossus" of South Africa, saying:

"But as to one thing I am perfectly convinced—that while the fault of Mr. Rhodes is about as great as a politician or a statesman can commit there has been nothing proved—and in my opinion there exists nothing—which affects Mr. Rhodes' personal position as a man of honour. . . . I dismiss absolutely these charges [stock-jobbing and the like] which affect his personal honour, and I find myself face to face with a statesman who has done the greatest service to the British Empire, but who has made one gigantic mistake."[24]

As Harcourt said, this remark by Chamberlain "effectively torpedoed the report of which he was a signatory." It also cast doubt as to Chamberlain's innocence in the raid itself as rumor spread that he vindicated Rhodes only because he had been forced to to prevent the disclosure of his own complicity.[25] Asquith in discussing the matter stated:

"This deliberate exculpation by the speaker of a man who, as the Report itself showed, had treated him atrociously seemed inexplicable except on the assumption of some threat held over Chamberlain's head."[26]

Was Chamberlain really involved?[27] The "Hawksley Letters,"[28] which were withheld from the Committee and the threat of publication of which were said to have caused his vindication of Rhodes, were no more damaging to him than the letters exchanged between Chamberlain and the permanent officials of the Colonial Office. It is a nice question but, according to a recognized authority,[29] it cannot be proved conclusively either way. While Chamberlain denied that he had anything to do with Jameson's *demarche,* he did admit to Flora Shaw that he did not desire full knowledge of the proceedings, saying:

"The fact is I can hardly say what I knew and what I did not. *I did not want to know too much.*[30] Of course I knew of the precautions, the preparations if you like, in view of the expected trouble in Johannesburg, but I never could have imagined that Jameson would take the bit in his teeth."[31]

In defending his actions before Parliament, Chamberlain had explained that the proceedings in Johannesburg and the Raid itself were two separate and disconnected events.[32] The two events were not, however, as disparate as Chamberlian would have had them appear. It has already been noted that he knew of the uprising which was to occur in Johannesburg, that he supported it and had made all the necessary arrangements to insure that British influence should prevail in the ensuing governmental organization. He even knew that Jameson was at Pitsani and planned that his men were to be used to strengthen the hand of the High Commissioner when he should proceed to Pretoria upon the outbreak of the revolt. Whether or not he was accountable for Jameson's foolish venture, he was, in part, answerable for the creation of the situation from which that act sprang.

As a responsible official of Her Majesty's Government he had connived at—and perhaps was even in collusion with—a conspiracy to overthrow the government of a friendly state. Aware that an uprising was being fomented in the Transvaal, he encouraged the progress of the plan instead of acting to prevent it. While his responsibility for Jameson's actions may not have been direct, it certainly was indirect. His attitude toward the conspiracy indicated to what lengths he was willing to go to further the extension of British rule in South Africa.

What were the interests of Britain that he was attempting to advance thereby? As Chamberlain himself said, the chief factor governing the situation in South Africa was "that Great Britain is, has been, and must continue to be the paramount Power in those [South African] regions."[33] In maintaining this primacy Chamberlain admitted that Great Britain ought to try to act in such a way as to preserve good feelings between the Dutch and the British living there. He was conscious of the fact that the raid had placed this neighborly feeling in some jeopardy.[34] He was also conscious of the fact that war between Great Britain and the Transvaal would be disastrous to the continued amicability of the two peoples, for he said on May 8, 1896:

"A war in South Africa would be one of the most serious wars that could possibly be waged. It would be in the nature of a civil war. It would be a long war, a bitter war, and a costly war and . . . it would leave behind it the embers of a strife which I believe generations would hardly be long enough to extinguish . . . To go to war with President Kruger in order to force upon him reforms in the internal affairs of his state . . . would have been a course of action as immoral as it would have been unwise."[35]

Considering Chamberlain's part in the abortive rebellion in Johannesburg, his remarks to a London audience, March 27, 1897, appear strangely incongrous. On that occasion he said:

". . . We, on our part, are ready, at all times, to extend to our Dutch fellow-subjects, with open hands, all the privileges which we enjoy ourselves, and . . . we have shown again and again by our declarations that we have no intention and no desire to interfere with the independence of neighboring States."[36]

In Chamberlain's attitude and action during this period one sees the spirit of a mature apostle of imperialism. Here there is no evidence of the growth of Empire "in a fit of absence of mind."[37] Neither is this the bombastic imperialism or Jingoism of a Palmerston or a Disraeli. This is imperialism coldly and maliciously schemed. The calculations, however, went awry which meant that, in the end, Chamberlain's purpose could only be accomplished by a war "as immoral as it . . . [was] unwise."

Chamberlain, now interested mainly in the extension of Empire, was instrumental in negotiating a treaty with France to define spheres of influence in West Africa. There the French, instigated by Premier

Hanatoux, sent out small contingents to occupy posts in areas in which neither English nor French titles were clear, although both claimed the territory. Chamberlain stole a leaf from Hanatoux's book and likewise organized expeditions to establish stations in the same areas. This gave England excellent grounds for bargaining when the negotiations took place, most of the disputed districts going to England.[38]

While Chamberlain was Colonial Secretary he often took an active part in the work of the Foreign Office, particularly regarding the possibilities of an alliance with the United States and Germany. While this is not the place for an extended treatment of this phase of Chamberlain's activity, it must be noted briefly. Just before the Jameson raid, President Cleveland in a message to Congress announced the appointment of an American Commission to settle the boundary dispute between Venezuela and British Guinea, the findings of the Commission to be enforced by the United States acting under the Monroe Doctrine. This caused deep resentment in England, soon overshadowed, however, by the animosity toward Germany aroused by the Kaiser's congratulatory message to President Kruger. In the Fall of 1896 Chamberlain and his wife visited her parents in America, Chamberlain taking this opportunity to talk with Secretary of State Olney regarding the dispute. At first Chamberlain thought Olney rather obstinate about the matter, but later found him quite cordial. On the basis of these conversations Salisbury instructed the British Ambassador at Washington to continue his efforts toward a settlement upon which both parties soon agreed.

A few weeks after these conversations Olney opened correspondence with Chamberlain regarding the advisability of joint Anglo-American protests against the Armenian atrocities. To Olney's suggestion Chamberlain replied:

"I am deeply sensible to the importance of such moral and incidental co-operation in the cause of humanity as is pointed out in your letter and I believe it would profoundly affect the relations between the two countries, and would evoke the sympathy, which, even if latent, must and ought to exist between peoples with common origin, common literature, common laws and common standards of right and wrong."[39]

Because of the common traits of the two peoples Chamberlain desired more cordial and intimate relations between the United States and Great Britain. He believed that:

". . . blood will be found to be thicker than water . . . [and] that the closer, the more definite, the clearer the alliance between the United States and ourselves, the better it will be for both nations, the better it will be for the civilized world, and the better it will be for all that we have a right to hope for."[40]

Chamberlain was also interested in securing an alliance with Germany and to this end carried on conversations with the German Ambassador, Hatzfeld, and with Baron Eckardstein, who was supposed to have the ear of Wilhelm II. These conversations came to nothing, but it is interesting to note that Chamberlain felt that any agreement between the two nations should stipulate that Great Britain was to have a free hand in the Transvaal.[41]

The "great dream" of the Colonial Secretary was to create a more closely knit Empire during his stay in office. It will be remembered that in 1886 and 1887 he declared that the self-governing colonies could not be forced to remain in the Empire against their wishes. He continued to hold this view throughout his life. In 1895 he declared that they had every necessary element of national life and had already taken their place among the nations of the world.[42] Two years later the self-governing colonies were, to him, no longer dependencies but kindred states.[43] As late as May 9, 1906, he said:

"They are nations rejoicing in their own independence. . . . They are no longer our dependents, but with us they own a common flag, they own with pride allegiance to a common authority in the presence of a common King, and otherwise and in their own affairs they are uncontrolled and supreme."[44]

Even though Chamberlain thought that Canada and Australia were independent states in all but name, he rejoiced at the circumstance that, as the possibilities for the disintegration of the Empire had increased, the desire for continued unity had also grown stronger. Of course, he felt that separation would have been calamitous since it would have meant a break with the traditions of the past which had "carried into every clime British institutions and the best characteristics of the British race."[45] Since certain of the colonies had become more or less independent, any scheme to draw the Empire into a more closely knit structure would have to take into consideration the opinions and the wishes of the colonists.[46] Regardless of the obstacles that impeded the fuller unity of Greater Britain, Chamberlain felt that it was to the interest of all to draw the bonds closer, for, as he declared at the Royal Colonial Institute dinner on March 31, 1897:

"It seems to me that the tendency of the time is to throw all power into the hands of the greater Empires, and the minor kingdoms—those which are non-progressive—seem to be destined to fall into a secondary and subordinate place. But, if Greater Britain remains united, no empire in the world can ever surpass it in area, in population, in wealth, or in the diversity of its resources."[47]

For these reasons and because he was concerned "for the future of the Anglo-Saxon people,"[48] he desired an Imperial Federation. The first concern of this federation he thought to be Imperial defense, but, as this would require a financial arrangement, he did not believe that the defense problems could be solved outside of a commercial union.[49] However, at that time (1896), Chamberlain was still defending the principles of free trade because he felt that the foreign trade of Great Britain was so much larger than the trade with the colonies that preferences within the Empire would not compensate for the loss in foreign trade which would result from such a preferential agreement.[50] Because he adhered to this principle he did not receive much consideration from the colonies.[51]

Always interested in Empire federation, Chamberlain welcomed the growing plans for a confederation of the Australian colonies into one federal union. The Australian colonies drew up their constitution and sent it to London with their representatives who were to supervise its passage through Parliament at Westminster. Chamberlain approved all the provisions in the constitution except the one dealing with the right of appeal from the Australian courts to the Judicial Committee of the Privy Council. According to this clause, the appeal would lie only in those instances in which Empire interests other than Australian were involved. While still maintaining that the ties binding Australia to Great Britain would include no obligation that the colony considered irksome, Chamberlain thought that the link ought to be stronger than that provided in the new constitution.[52] Accordingly, he negotiated strenuously with the Australian delegates for a change in the clause, and made a direct appeal to the colonial governments in Australia. Finally he broke down the unanimous opposition of the delegates and was able to force through a compromise which provided that appeal should lie to the Privy Council in all cases save those in which Australian interests exclusively were involved.[53] With this compromise, the Constitution of Australia Bill was passed without further difficulty, and the Queen signed it on June 9, 1900.

The only difference between the right of appeal placed in the Australian Constitution and the right of appeal desired by the Australian delegates was that, in the latter instance, the colony would have had some voice in deciding what was local and what was Imperial in nature, while in the appeal clause as finally inserted Great Britain was to have the authority. This was an illustration of Chamberlain's desire to give Great Britain the paramount control over all the self-governing colonies.[54] While he admitted—or seemed to—that the self-governing colonies were practically independent, he also wanted to bring the colonies closer to Great Britain. This desire outweighed any inclination he may have had to allow those colonies to go their own way and led him to work strenuously and effectively to hold Australia in check.

It has already been noted on several occasions that Chamberlain took great pride in the Anglo-Saxon race and its superior qualities, which peculiarly fitted the British people for their supposed mission of civilization. He combined pride of race with the notion of the duty of Great Britain to carry the benefits of European culture to "backward people." Thus we find Chamberlain, in 1895, saying:

"I believe that the British race is the greatest governing race that the world has ever seen. I say this not merely as an empty boast, but as proved and evidenced by the success which we have had in administering the vast dominions which are connected with these small islands."[55]

In 1897 he rejoiced that civilization had been advanced because of expansion:

"I do not say that all our methods have been beyond reproach but I do say that in almost every instance in which the rule of the Queen has been established and the great *Pax Britannica* has been enforced, there has come with it greater security to life and property, and a material improvement in the bulk of the population. No doubt in the first instance, when these conquests have been made, there has been bloodshed, there has been loss of life among the natives, loss of still more precious lives amongst those who have been sent out to bring those countries into some kind of disciplined order, but it must be remembered that that is the condition of the mission we have to fulfil . . . but . . . we may rest assured that for one life lost a hundred will be gained, and the cause of civilisation and the prosperity of the people will in the long run be eminently advanced."[56]

In his estimation Great Britain had a duty to perform:

"We have to carry civilization, British justice, British law, religion and Christianity to millions and millions, to people who until our advent had lived in ignorance, in bitter conflict, and whose territories have fallen to us to develop. That is our duty. It is our great duty. It removes altogether from us the reproach of selfishness, of parochial politics."[57]

One could continue to quote endless statements of a similar character; two more on racial superiority, however, should suffice:

"Let the Little Englanders say what they like, we are a great governing race, predestined by our defects, as well as by our virtues to spread over the habitable globe and to enter into relations with all the countries of the earth."[58]

". . . We alone among the nations of the earth have been able to establish and maintain colonies under different conditions in all parts of the world, we have maintained them to their own advantage and to ours, and we have secured not only the loyal attachment of all British subjects but the general goodwill of the races whether they be native or whether they be European that have come under the British flag."59

With Disraeli, who began this period of British imperialism, one of the primary motivating factors seems to have been his love of the "pomp and circumstance" of Empire. But with Chamberlain it was a belief in the superiority of the British race and its mission to civilize the "backward" peoples of the globe. His reasoning that the British were the greatest governing race the world had ever seen was based on an argument after the fact. He did not say that because the British were the greatest of governing people they spread over the globe; rather he said because they expanded over such a wide area they were the most able race. He also stated that their greatness could be seen in the success that they had enjoyed in administering their vast domains. Without stopping to examine his particular idea of "success," it may not be amiss to point out that that success might have been the result of experience acquired over a long period of dealing with various native races rather than any inherent qualities in the British themselves. That same experience might easily have been acquired by any other people over a like period of time under similar circumstances.

Although in spreading the benefits of civilization all the methods of the British were not above reproach, Chamberlain claimed nevertheless that the end had justified the means. It ought to be remembered, however, that the means modify and temper the ends. If the means employed are brutal and crude the end itself is not likely to be free of brutality and crudity. In Chamberlain's estimation British expansion had brought with it a greater security of life and property. No doubt he was thinking in terms of British life and British property or, at most, in terms of the life and property of Europeans. These were, of course, more secure as the result of that expansion, but the effects of expansion have to be judged in terms of the total product. What of native life and native property? Was that more secure? Before the British came the lives and property of one tribe of natives were subject to attack from another tribe. But it must be remembered that the weapons of the one tribe were similar to the weapons of the other. The tribes were, at least, rather evenly matched. It is true the British put an end to inter-tribal warfare. But having put an end to that, they then proceeded to take the native's property. When he resisted they took his life with greater ease and dispatch than had his native enemies since their European weapons were superior. Having occupied a part of the territory, the British usually promised to protect the natives in the rest but when the British settlers wanted some of the remaining territory they usually took it. True, it was all done "legally", that is, the chieftain signed (often under duress or misrepresentation) a treaty allowing the British to come in and occupy the land; nevertheless the idea that all property and all lives had greater security after the British assumed control is open to question.

Was there any material improvement for the bulk of the population? In Africa the wage-scale of the natives working in the mines was infinitely lower than the wages paid to the Europeans; this differential was maintained in order to prevent the natives from bettering their material condition since improvement might well have meant a change in the social status of the natives. Moreover, the Europeans, although a decided minority, rigidly excluded the natives from participation in political activity for fear that some of the privileges of the Europeans might have been endangered thereby. It is difficult to see that much general progress for the native population could be possible under such conditions. Was this conferring the benefits of civilization upon the natives? In India where, undoubtedly, the natives were more intellectually developed than the Africans, the Indians were excluded from all but the lesser administrative offices. If the civilizing process is to be judged in terms of native development of democracy it is difficult to agree that the English policy was a civilizing one. The expansionist policy may well have been advantageous to the British themselves; whether it profited the natives may be questioned. It probably resulted in the adoption by the natives of the ways of European culture not necessarily because they liked it, but because they found that only by so doing could they resist the advances of the Europeans and, ultimately, restore control over native territory to the natives themselves.

The excerpts from Chamberlain's speeches given above well illustrate his conviction that "Sentiment is one of the greatest factors in all our affairs . . . the world is not governed by interest, or in my opinion, particularly by interest."[60] Reasons of sentiment seemed to have governed practically all of Chamberlain's activities in the field of imperialism. He had opposed Irish Home Rule out of attachment for the preservation of the unity of the Empire; he desired the expansion of the Empire because of his belief in the peculiar fitness of the British people to colonize and civilize the "backward" areas of the world. It is true that he dwelt on economic arguments when he developed his plan for tariff reform, but even there, as will be noted in the following chapter,[61] he evolved his scheme in order to strengthen the bonds which held the Empire together. The material economic factors were, to him, secondary; reasons of sentiment were paramount. The emotional drive toward imperialism appeared also in his efforts to expand the British Empire in those areas where other powers seemed likely to plant their flags. Most writers on the theory of imperialism, exclusive of the Marxists, stress emotional and sentimental factors of this sort as important causes, although they usually locate the prime factor leading to imperialism within the economic framework of society. Chamberlain subordinated the economic factor to the sentimental factor. However, this did not mean that the British policy of imperialism under Chamberlain was a thing of "sweetness and light". It did not mean that the policy was any less brutal or any less vicious than it would have been if the driving force behind it were more material. Individuals and groups often engage in rather reprehensible practices under the illusion that by so doing they advance the cause of religion, civilization or some other "good" cause. So-called Christians have in the past burned "heretics" at the stake, being convinced that they furthered Christianity thereby. It is not suggested here that Chamberlain was a fanatic, but ideas similar to his in the hands of a fanatic may result in the brutalization of whole peoples. One needs only to examine casually the result of Hitler's policies to be convinced of this.

Chamberlain's feeling regarding racial pride and the mission of the British people was similar to those expressed by other British imperialists of the time. Lord Curzon dedicated his book on the Far East "To those who believe that the British Empire is under Providence the greatest instrument for good that the world has seen."[62] Milner in his book on Egypt said of the British task there:

"Alike by the nature of our interests, by the nature of our power, and by certain special qualities in our national character, we seem marked out for the discahrge of this particular duty."[63]

Lord Rosebery, leader of the Liberal imperialists, had expressed his views along parrallel lines. Cecil Rhodes,[64] with his inordinate desire to paint the map red, had views which approximated those quoted above, although he stressed the "divine" mission more than his associates.

A contrary view of Empire had been expressed earlier by Jonathan Swift in his *Gulliver's Travels*:

"'A crew of pirates, he says, are driven by a storm, they know not whither; at length a boy discovers land from the topmast; they go on shore to rob and plunder; they see a harmless people, are entertained with kindness; they give the country a new name; they take formal possession of it for their king; they set up a rotten plank or stone for a memorial; they murder two or three dozen of the natives, bring away a couple more by force for a sample, return home, and get their pardon. Here commences a new dominion, acquired with a title by divine right. Ships are sent with the first opportunity; the natives driven out or destroyed; their princes tortured to discover their gold; a free license given to all acts of inhumanity and lust; the earth reeking with the blood of its inhabitants; and this execrable crew of butchers employed in so pious an expedition is a modern colony sent out to convert and civilise an idolatrous and barbarous people.'"[65]

Chamberlain's views on British racial superiority were quite common at that time. Someone has said that when Darwin enunciated his ideas on evolution he interpreted that phenomenon in the light of two distinctive attributes of the British people, struggle and adaptation. While this facetious remark may be disregarded, it is certain that after the appearance of *The Origin of Species* and *The Descent of Man,* Darwin's interpretation of biological evolution was, contrary to his warning, used in the interpretation of social and historical processes. There was much talk then—as there is now—concerning the superiority of one race over another, despite the fact that no criteria have ever been devised to prove this. Since the fittest were to survive, the proponents of social Darwinism were unwilling to be too humanitarian in their treatment of the "backward" races since to do so would allow a weak race to survive and eventually affect the superior. The extermination or the subjection of the weaker races was a necessary incident in the struggle for the survival of the fitttest and was to be welcomed on that account.

Chamberlain, as has been previously noted, was influenced in his desire to extend the Empire by his wish to circumvent other states in their plans to acquire more territory and by his belief that the future would be dominated by the largest and the strongest empires.[66] Whenever Chamberlain heard that another country was thinking of establishing control over some bit of territory hitherto unclaimed by a Western nation his practice was to get there first and establish British control. It was impossible to do this in all cases; he probably regretted that it was impossible to declare a universal British protectorate over all areas in which European states had not yet planted their flags. Whether this obsession resulted from an intense chauvinism or from his belief in the superiority of the English it is difficult to say. There can be no doubt that he had this belief, and had had it apparently when he first entered politics. Even when he had been interested chiefly in local politics and social reform this attitude was quite prominent. It was natural that this penchant should have been intensified in the nineties when international rivalries began to make themselves increasingly felt. These rivalries which sprang up in the last years of the nineteenth century as a result of a desire for colonies, "a place in the sun," greater power, and added prestige resulted naturally in an increase in sea and land armaments. It was the beginning of the politics of power that culminated in the World War. The chief participants in this game of *Machtpolitik* were England, France, Germany, and Russia. Japan was just beginning her career, but was not regarded seriously by the European states until after the Russo-Japanese War. As Chamberlain saw these rivalries grow he sensed that the history of the future would be determined by the interplay of these larger states. Since he believed that the British race was superior to all others, that they were better colonial administrators than their rivals, and that they had a mission to carry the benefits of European civilization to "backward" areas, he wanted Great Britain to be the strongest and the greatest of the great powers and the chief influence in the history of the future.

It is quite interesting to note the change in emphasis that occurred in Chamberlain's attitude toward domestic and foreign politics. Prior to 1886 he had been chiefly interested in domestic reform, but in 1897, answering John Morley's charge that the Salisbury Government had done nothing good, he declared:

"They [the Radicals] forget, in the attention which they give to these domestic controversies, which, after all, whichever way they are settled, are of minor importance—they forget the great part which the country has played, and is called upon to play, in the history of the world. I say that this is the fatal mistake which alienates from men, otherwise influential and worthy of admiration, the sympathies of the great mass of their countrymen."[67]

Chamberlain rejoiced that the masses of the people were taking an interest in foreign and Imperial affairs.[68] He declared that he believed that the working classes had always put the welfare of the Empire before all else.[69] It will be remembered that in his campaign speeches of 1885 he had stated that the masses would never be interested in a policy of expansion and aggression. But with his Imperial ideas in full bloom any question that did not concern the whole of the Empire ought, in Chamberlain's estimation, not be given too much serious consideration.[70] For to devote too much attention to local affairs would be to return to the position of Little Englanderism which would place Britain at the mercy of any foreign nation.[71]

While Chamberlain was giving voice to his views on Imperial policy he was not idle in his actions tending to further the extension of the Empire and the maintenance of British priority in South Africa. His chief concern here was to seek guarantees from Germany that she would not interfere with any action which Great Britain might take with regard to the Transvaal. His first opportunity in this respect came in 1898 as a result of negotiations with Portugal for a loan to pay the expected damages resulting from the impending Berne Award. In 1883 Portugal, proprietor of Delagoa Bay and its port Lorenco Marques, the chief sea outlet of the Transvaal, had granted a concession to an American engineer, MacMurdo, to build a railroad from the port of Pretoria. This project the British capitalists financed. In 1889 Portugal seized the railway. Great Britain and the United States protested and the matter was referred to a group of Swiss jurists for settlement. It was expected that the award would be in favor of the protesting governments and that Portugal would be compelled to pay heavy damages. Portugal, thinking it would not be able to finance the payment, negotiated with Great Britain to back the necessary loan. When arrangements were almost completed, Germany lodged a demand to be included as a joint guarantor of the loan. Chamberlain agreed to this, providing that Germany should consent to remain neutral respecting the Transvaal. So an agreement was made, but the award proved to be less than expected and Portugal succeeded in paying the damages without calling on England and Germany. Thus the treaty became a dead letter.[72]

The next opportunity came in the following year when war was a practical certainty. Great Britain and Germany both had claims to Samoa and had agreed to administer the territory jointly with the United States, which also had claims. Joint administration did not work well and when, about this time, a dispute arose over the succession of the native chieftainship; Germany and Great Britain backed opposing candidates. Some settlement had to be made. Germany desired to keep her hold on Samoa since that represented one of her first colonial ventures. Great Britain wanted to keep a foothold there because of the interests of Australia. The Kaiser, however, demanded Samoa as the price of Germany's neutrality in the forthcoming Transvaal War. Chamberlain, believeing the Transvaal question to be of greater importance than any other, advised the Prime Minister to pay blackmail in this instance.[73] The agreement giving up Somoa was then signed and the German Emperor visited England during Cowes Week as a sign of his neutrality in the Transvaal struggle.[74]

The chief issue arising out of the Transvaal troubles, as Chamberlain saw it, was the necessity of maintaining the British lead in South Africa. The Boers had always wanted complete independence, which Great Britain had refused to grant. As has been mentioned earlier, the Boers denied citizenship to the Uitlanders except after a lengthy period of residence. For a time Chamberlain pinned some hope on the possibility that the reform party in the Transvaal might defeat Kruger, who represented the *status quo* group of the Boers, but when Kruger was re-elected in 1898, that door was firmly shut.

Events moved rapidly after this. In December of 1898, Edgar, an English subject engaged as a mine worker, returning to his home in Johannesburg under the influence of liquor, became engaged in a brawl with several Boers during which he knocked one of his opponents to the ground and proceeded to his home nearby. When the police came Edgar refused to open his door and was shot. This act stirred up immense resentment in England which was heightened when the policeman was released at the trial in Johannesburg.

A few months later, several thousand Uitlanders who were British subjects drew up a petition to the Queen, asking for aid in the settlement of the franchise question. The British Government accepted the petition— in itself a fact which irked the Boers, who thought Great Britain had no right to interfere. The result of this petition was the calling of a conference between Kruger and the High Commissioner to South Africa, now Sir Alfred Milner, to settle the matter. The conference met in Blomfontein in the Orange Free State. Kruger proposed to grant the franchise after seven years residence within the Transvaal, the measure not to be retroactive; Milner held out for a five-year retroactive franchise. No agreement being possible, the conference broke up on June 5, 1899. But prospects for settlement brightened in July when Chamberlain learned that the Transvaal planned to introduce a measure providing for a seven-year retroactive franchise. However, this soon proved futile, due to Kruger's demands that upon the extension of the franchise Great Britain was to promise not to interfere in Transvaal affairs, not to insist on Transvaal suzerainty, and to agree to arbitration.[75] This would have meant recognition of the Transvaal as an independent state, a step Chamberlain would not take because of his insistence that Great Britain continue to be the paramount power.

On September 21, 1899, Chamberlain rejected these demands, and the Boers prepared for war. The British Government did likewise, the Cabinet meeting on October 9 to dispatch an ultimatum to Kruger, but the following morning Chamberlain received news that Kruger had sent in his ultimatum that the British withdraw their troops from the borders immediately. This the Cabinet rejected; hostilities commenced October 12, 1899, and lasted until March of 1901. This study is not concerned with the details of the war;[76] is is concerned, however, with Chamberlain's attitude toward the war and the lessons he seemed to see in it.

Chamberlain undoubtedly hoped that his policies regarding the Transvaal could be carried out without recourse to war, but after the failure of the Blomfontein Conference he pursued a policy "of thinly veiled menace,"[77] which led ultimately to war when the Boers refused to be intimidated. Chamberlain showed that he was losing his patience with the Boers in June, 1899, when he said that forbearance was becoming a sign of weakness and that the British were losing their self-respect by continuing to be patient.[78] Later he said that he had no intention of interfering with the independence of the Boers; he merely wanted to make that independence secure by relieving the discontented Uitlanders.[79]

On October 19, 1899, after the war had begun, he defined the principles for which Great Britain was fighting in South Africa. The first was the protection of British subjects. The second was the determination that Great Britian should remain the paramount power in South Africa. When he said that, he limited South Africa to include only the British possessions there plus the two Republics. On this occasion he referred to a speech he had made earlier—in 1896—when he had said that war in South Africa would be immoral and unwise. He pointed out in extenuation that he had not said that war would always be immoral and unwise.[80]

He stated further that the Boers as a race were contemptuous of the English. It was his belief that as long as this feeling lasted peace was impossible. He thought that peace could only come after the Boers had been taught to respect the English, which the war would do.[81] To have refused to go to war with the Boers would have meant, in his estimation, a destruction of the influence of the Empire, the loss of control over India. It would also have made Great Britain ridiculous in the eyes of the civilized world. For these reasons the war to him was inevitable.[82] To Chamberlain the war was "a just, a righteous, and a necessary" one.[83] It was a contest to determine whether the British people or the Boers were to be the chief influence in South African affairs.[84] He declared also that he was willing to assume personal responsibility for the war.[85]

Reginald I. Lovell, a recognized authority, has said that the real reasons which prompted Great Britain to go to war were the hope that the Transvaal would return to Great Britain sooner or later, coupled with the fear that if the Uitlanders were given the vote, a South African federation might crystallize around the South African Republic rather than around the Cape Government.[86] Milner's opinion was that war was the only course available to save the British Empire in South Africa.[87] This war, for which Chamberlain had accepted personal responsibility, was a war of wanton aggression, comparable to the Italian rape of Ethiopia, brought about by Chamberlain's overwhelming desire to see Great Britain the "top dog" in South Africa. When Austen Chamberlain was Chancellor of the Exchequer for the second time, a memorandum came to his hand characterizing the South African War as one of aggression. He noted in the margin: "Possibly, but you should not say so to my father's son."[88]

When it became apparent that Great Britain would go to war with the Transvaal, Chamberlain hoped that the self-governing colonies would send contingents of troops so that the war would appear to be truly an Imperial one. Australia was the first to meet his desire by offering troops as early as July, 1899, three months before the war actually began. Offers of troops from Malaya, Trinidad, and Hongkong were declined because of racial differences. Chamberlain wanted it to be exclusively a white man's war, no natives need apply.[89] Canada, because of the differences between the French and the English inhabitants, was reluctant to send any troops. Chamberlain did not want to appear to request soldiers from Canada but he exerted strong indirect pressure on the Canadian Government which caused them to agree on October 14, 1899.[90] With all the colonies thus co-operating, Chamberlain's hope that the Empire would be united "shoulder to shoulder"[91] was finally realized.

To Chamberlain, regardless of the cost of the war, it had been more than compensated for by the fact that it had demonstrated the strength and unity of the Empire.[92] It had, as he said in 1902:

". . . enabled the British Empire to find itself; it has united the British race throughout the world, and it has shown to all whom it may concern that if ever we have, as we have done in the past, to fight for our very existence against a world in arms, we shall not be alone. We shall be supported by the sons of Britain in every part of the globe."[93]

Because of the rebirth of a feeling of common interests among the members of the Empire Chamberlain hoped that a federative movement would be organized to give realistic expression to the unity of the Empire.[94]

One of the minor reasons for going to war with the Transvaal had been, said Chamberlain, to rescue the native population from barbarous treatment.[95]Admitting that this was in itself a worthy motive, Chamberlain's native policy was not of the best and he certainly might have been attacked for it. In 1898 the natives in Sierre Leon revolted when a hut tax of five shillings was imposed. Chamberlain appointed Sir David Chalmers to investigate conditions there; Chalmers' report indicated that the revolt was due to the imposition of the tax which, in reality, resulted in a thinly veiled form of slavery. Despite this report, Chamberlain continued in his insistence that the hut tax be retained.[96] Chamberlain defended his stand in Parliament on the ground that the hut tax in Sierre Leon was no greater than similar taxes in the French colony nearby.[97] He also indicated that he favored the tax as an indirect means to induce the natives to work,[98] thus indicating his approval of disguised slavery. Chamberlain refrained from calling it that and in fact denied it, but he also said that it was necessary to use indirect means to compel the natives to work.[99] It is difficult to see that there is any difference between forced labor and labor induced by indirect means such as the hut taxes. In defending the use of native labor in the mines and the taxes by which they were forced to work there, Chamberlain said that white men could not be expected to work for the cheap wages which the mine owners paid, hence the natives were to be compelled to work in order that the mines might produce a profit.[100] Chamberlain spoke also of the necessity of inculcating the natives with a respect for the dignity of labor but Kier Hardie replied that it was difficult to censure the native for not working since the dignity of labor even in England meant no more than long hours of work, low wages, and the privilege of living in the slums.[101]

Chamberlain also defended the immigration of indentured coolie laborers into South Africa and expressed his disapproval of the action of India in refusing to allow the emigration of Indian natives as indentured laborers. These coolies would not interfere with the Kaffir labor since the Kaffirs would be working underground while the coolies did surface work. Chamberlain stated that the coolies would not be allowed to remain in South Africa for longer that the period of their indentured service, thus they would not complicate the race problem in that region. His contention was that the coolies would be helped by the labor since they would be able to return to their homes richly rewarded for their short stay.[102]

There was room for doubting that Chamberlain's contentions regarding the Kaffir laborers and the coolies were valid. The Kaffir laborers could not pay their hut tax by working in their villages since the tax was more than they could make from the sale of agricultural produce. This forced them to work in the mines, which was the purpose of the hut tax. In working in the mines, they were herded together far away from their homes and their accustomed routine. Returning after an absence during which they had been subject to all the evil influences incidental to their labor, they often found it difficult to enter into their former tribal life. The same was true of the imported coolies; after a long separation from their families and their homes they could not return and take up life where had left it before going to Africa. The difficulties incidental to the English mission of civilizing "barbarous and idolatrous" natives were probably greater than Chamberlain visualized. His policy was hardly a credit to the "civilizing" mission of the British race.

Chamberlain became the object of parliamentary attacks as the war dragged on in 1900. He had said that the war was waged to strengthen the independence of the Boers but under his direction the Boers were disenfranchised. This called forth caustic comment from Lloyd George and other Liberals. Chamberlain even desired to disenfranchise the Boers of the Cape Colony because of their sympathy with their fellow-countrymen in the South African Republic.[103] This attitude seemed to many inconsistent with his remarks on the purposes of the war.

The attacks on Chamberlain's policy did not stop with mere objections to his actions in South Africa, however. Lloyd George accused him of desiring a protracted war so that his family could make a fortune out of governmental contracts. In his opening remarks Lloyd George reminded Parliament that Chamberlain, in laying down rules for the civil servants under him, had forbidden them or their families to hold shares of stock in land or even to own property in Ceylon because of speculative opportunities in land in that area. Lloyd George also pointed out that Chamberlain had opposed the appointment of

Sir Hercules Robinson as High Commissioner in South Africa because
he had held stock in one of Rhodes's concerns before his appointment,
although he held no such stock at the time of his appointment.[104]
Lloyd George then proceeded to outline the interest of the Chamberlains in companies which did business with the government. There
was the Colombo Commercial Company of Ceylon in which Chamberlain had 7,000 pounds invested. This firm had formerly been engaged
in coffee-planting exclusively but when the coffee trade failed the
company engaged in all types of speculation in Ceylon. Later, said
Lloyd George, when the accommodations for the war prisoners at
St. Helena became inadequate, the Government decided to send them
to Ceylon, selecting the Colombo Commercial Company to build the
necessary accommodations. Lloyd George also showed that Hoskins
and Sons, contractors to the Admiralty, was chiefly owned by Neville
Chamberlain, although Austen Chamberlain, who had been Civil Lord
of the Admiralty prior to his taking a position in the Treasury, owned
stock to the value of 3,000 pounds. Three other members of Chamberlain's family owned the remainder of the stock with the exception of
a few shares held by clerks who were dummy shareholders with one
share each. The law required that a limited company have at least
seven shareholders, but Hoskins had increased this number to ten,
which seemed to Lloyd George a device to circumvent another law
which prevented any member of Parliament from sharing in a concern
which had business with the Government unless there were at least
ten shareholders.

Another charge related to Tubes, Ltd., which before 1899 had
been engaged in the manufacture of tubes for cycles. This had not
proved a profitable business, with losses at around 4,000 pounds
annually. In that year, however, Arthur Chamberlain, the Colonial
Secretary's brother, bought a controlling interest in the company, the
other members of the family and Jesse Collins doing likewise. As soon
as the Chamberlains had invested in this stock its value rose. Arthur
Chamberlain, when he assumed control, changed the nature of the
business and began to manufacture tubes for use in the boilers of the
ships of Her Majesty's Navy.

Lloyd George continued the tell-tale list. About 50 per cent of
the stock, acquired since 1898, in the Eliot Metal Company was in
the hands of the Chamberlain family—almost 125,000 pounds. This
company, as well as the two mentioned above advertised themselves
as contractors to the Admiralty and as companies possesing the con-

fidence of Her Majesty's Government, an advertisement likely to be taken seriously by those who knew the connection between the Chamberlain family and the Government. Chamberlain's brother controlled the Birmingham Small Arms Company also. This company manufactured cycle parts. When the War Office invited tenders for cycles it insisted that nine tenths of the parts in the cycles be manufactured by the Birmingham Small Arms Company.

Still another case was cited by Lloyd George. The Chamberlain family had invested in Kynoch and Company, manufacturers of cordite, to the extent of 250,000 pounds; Arthur Chamberlain ran this concern too. When the Government asked for bids in 1898, the National Explosive Company had sent one at six shillings less to the pound than Kynoch's asked. Several other companies had also sent in bids lower than that of the Kynoch company. The Admiralty, instead of awarding the contract to the lowest bidder, requested Kynoch's to resubmit its bid at the same figure as that of the National Explosive Company. This done, the Admiralty gave Kynoch's contract for over half of the needed cordite, the National Explosive Company receiving a contract for the remainder. None of the other companies who submitted bids lower than that of Kynoch's was given an opportunity to resubmit their bids. In 1900 the contract for the supply of cordite again went to Kynoch's and the National Explosive Company under similar circumstances, despite the fact that the inspectors reported that the cordite manufactured by Kynoch's was the poorest of the various samples tested and that much of their product had to be rejected because of its poor quality.

Lloyd George's purpose in bringing this information to the attention of the House was, of course, to accuse Chamberlain of using his influence to secure profitable contracts for these concerns, a practice Lloyd George thought unsuitable to a member of the Cabinet. Chamberlain denied that he had used his influence in any improper way. He disclaimed responsibility for the actions of his relatives and argued that the companies in question grew because of the business ability of his family rather than because of any favoritism due to his position.[105]

It seems logical to believe, however, that he would not have to put any pressure on the War Office or the Admiralty Office to compel them to offer contracts to companies which the Chamberlain family controlled. The War Office and the Admiralty Office, knowing that the Chamberlain family had heavily invested in certain firms, would naturally be inclined to favor those concerns above their competitors.

Chamberlain's personal intervention was unnecessary. This does not imply that he was interested in prolonging the war for personal gain to himself and to his family. The fact that the Chamberlain family began investing heavily in munitions in 1898 seems to indicate that they saw an opportunity to make a handsome profit out of the forthcoming war. In this they had the advantage of the "inside" information of the Colonial Secretary who at least anticipated, if he did not promote, the war. Thus the family was enabled to buy into these concerns at a reasonably low price; the advance in the value of the stock with the coming of the war made the investment doubly valuable. Whether Chamberlain and his family derived a corrupt profit from the war is a matter of opinion; it is something which, like his complicity in the Jameson Raid, cannot be proved or disproved.

When Lord Roberts occupied Pretoria in June of 1900 the popularity of the Government was somewhat restored, after being badly shaken by the earlier reverses in battle and by other criticism of its conduct of the war, such as the poor medical facilities and the tampering with military dispatches. Chamberlain, who was the driving force in the Cabinet in this period, decided to call an election immediately to take advantage of the swell of popular feeling, even though the term of Parliament lacked less than a year of being at an end. Although the conduct of the war had been criticized, the Government received a majority, perhaps due to the fact that the people feared the Liberals would make peace immediately if they had succeeded in winning the election. Lloyd George stated that in his estimation the haste with which Chamberlain called the election was a condemnation of the war by one who gloried in the fact that he commenced it.[106]

In the Autumn of 1902 Chamberlain journeyed to South Africa to plead for a healing of the wounds of the war. While there his remarks showed a definite tinge of social Darwinism. He spoke of the inevitable struggle for supremacy between the Britons and the Boers. Now that the struggle was over all knew which was the fitter race. He felt assured that since the Boers knew which was superior they would accept the results of the war and co-operate with the British in making a South African federation possible.[107]

REFERENCES

[1]Garvin, *op. cit.*, III, 4-5.
[2]*Ibid.*, 15-6.
[3]*Ibid.*, 169-70.
[4]*For. & Col. Speeches, op. cit.*, 50-1.
[5]*Ibid.*, 67.

6*Ibid.*, 66. In the speech as recorded in *Hansard* the clerk interpolated the fact that ironical cheers were heard after this remark.

7*Ibid.*, 52-66.

8Speech of Chamberlain reported in *The Times,* November 16, 1898.

9Garvin, *op. cit.*, 236.

10Cmd. 7918, 1896, p. 99.

11*Cf.* Hobson, *op. cit.*, passim.

12Garvin, *op. cit.*, 44.

13W. L. Langer, *The Diplomacy of Imperialism* (New York, 1935), I, 238.

14Garvin, *op. cit.*, 48.

15Robinson to Chamberlain, *ibid.*, 59-62.

16*Ibid.*, 63.

17*Ibid.*, 72.

18*Ibid.*, 73.

19*Ibid.*, 74.

20*Ibid.*, 79.

21*Ibid.*, 82.

22Complete details of the raid and the correspondence relating thereto may be found in Cmd. 7933, 1896, "Correspondence on Recent Disturbances . . . "

23Garvin, *op. cit.*, 101.

24*Hansard,* 4th. Ser., v. 51, p. 1172.

25Gardiner, *Harcourt,* II, 436.

26J. A. Spender & Cyril Asquith, *The Life of Herbert Henry Asquith, Lord of Oxford and Asquith* (London, 1932), I, 131.

27See F. C. Gould, *Political Caricatures* (London, 1903).

28Quoted in Garvin, *op. cit.*, 110-11.

29R. I. Lovell, *The Struggle for South Africa* (New York, 1934), 320-1.

30The italics are the author's.

31Garvin, *op. cit.*, 83.

32*Hansard,* 4th. Ser., v. 37, p. 309.

33*For. & Col. Speeches, op. cit.*, 205.

34*Hansard,* 4th. Ser., v. 40, p. 907.

35*Ibid.*, 914-5.

36*For. & Col. Speeches, op. cit.*, 223.

37J. R. Seeley, *Expansion of England* (London, 1883), 81.

38For full details see Garvin, *op. cit.*, ch. LV.

39*Ibid.*, 168.

40*Hansard,* 4th. Ser., v. 58, p. 1438.

41For details of the conversations see Garvin, *op. cit.*, ch. LVIII.

42*The Times,* November 7, 1895.

43Boyd, *op. cit.*, II, 2.

44Quoted in *The Times,* May 9, 1906.

45Quoted, *ibid.*, November 7, 1895.

46*Ibid.*, January 13, 1902; Boyd, *op. cit.*, II, 133.

47Boyd, *op. cit.*, I, 4-5.

48Quoted in *The Times,* November 7, 1895.

49*For. & Col. Speeches,* 166.

50Boyd, *op. cit.*, I, 370.

51Chamberlain's plan for the commercial federation of the Empire will be discussed in detail in the next chapter.

52*Hansard,* 4th. Ser., v. 83, p. 74.

53*Ibid.*, v.84, p. 338.

54*Ibid.*, 766.

55*For. & Col. Speeches, op. cit.*, 89; see also Boyd, *op. cit.*, II, 300, for a similar statement.

56*Ibid.*, II, 3-4.

57Quoted in *The Times,* January 7, 1902; see also *ibid.*, January 14, 1902.

58Quoted, *ibid.*, January 30, 1897.

59Quoted, *ibid.*, January 22, 1896; see also *ibid.*, January 30, 1899; Boyd, *op. cit.*, II, 298.

60Quoted in Petrie, *op. cit.*, 41.

61*Vide, infra.,* 109-13.

62George Curzon, *Problems of the Far East* (London, 1894).

63A. Milner, *England in Egypt* (London, 1892), 435-6.

64Here is an example of Rhodes' mystical devotion to imperialism: "If there be a God and He cares anything about what I do, I think it is clear that He would like me to do what He is doing himself. And as He is manifestly fashioning the English-speaking race as the chosen instrument by which He will bring in a state of Society based upon Justice, Liberty and Peace, He must obviously wish me to do what I can to give as much scope and power to that race as possible."

65This opinion is similar to that expressed by George Bernard Shaw in the preface to *Arms and the Man,* in which he gives the following picture of John Bull: "As the great champion of freedom and independence he conquers half the world and calls it Colonization. When he wants a new market for his adulterated goods, he sends a missionary to teach the natives the gospel of peace. The natives kill the missionary; he flies to arms in defense of Chrisianity; fights for it, conquers for it; and takes the market as a reward from heaven. . . ."

66See his speeches quoted in *The Times,* November 25, 1897; January 19, 1898.

67*For. & Col. Speeches, op. cit.,* 235.

68*The Times,* May 14, 1898.

69J. Chamberlain, *Imperial Union and Tariff Reform* (London, 1903), 130; Boyd, *op. cit.,* II, 372.

70*Ibid.,* 127-8.

71*Ibid.,* 140.

72For details see Garvin, *op. cit.,* 307-23.

73*Ibid.,* 335.

74*Ibid.,* 343.

75*Ibid.,* 437.

76The best general treatment may be found in Eric A. Walker, *A History of South Africa* (London, 1928).

77Spender & Asquith, *op. cit.,* I, 132.

78*The Times,* June 27, 1899.

79*Hansard,* 4th. Ser., v. 75, p. 698.

80Boyd, *op. cit.,* 20-22.

81*Ibid.,* 24.

82*The Times,* November 30, 1899; January 12, 1904.

83*Hansard,* 4th. Ser., v. 78, p. 617.

84*Ibid.,* v. 89, p. 434.

85*Ibid.,* v. 78, p. 612.

86Lovell, *op. cit.,* 422.

87Cecil Headlam (ed.), *The Milner Papers* (London, 1931-33), II, 38.

88Petrie, *op. cit.,* 24.

89Garvin, *op cit.,* III, 465.

90*Ibid.,* 528-33.

91Quoted in *The Times,* August 28, 1899.

92Boyd, *op. cit.,* 66; 132-3.

93Quoted in *The Times,* February 13, 1902; see also *ibid.,* October 25, 1900.

94Boyd, *op. cit.,* 71.

95*Ibid.,* 25.

96Cmd., 8922, 1898; Cmd. p. 9388, 1899.

97*Hansard,* 4th Ser., v. 76, p. 126-9.

98*Ibid.,* v. 98, p. 1503.

99*Ibid.,* v. 112, p. 47.

100*Ibid.,* v. 119, p. 1281.

101*Ibid.,* v. 120, p. 100-12.

102*The Times,* May 6, 1905.

103*Hansard,* 4th. Ser., v. 86, p. 1200 ff.

104The source for this and for the following material on Chamberlain's pecuniary interest in the war is *Hansard,* 4th Ser., v. 88, p. 399-424.

105*Ibid.,* p. 441-8; v. 87, p. 1014.

106*Ibid.,* v. 86, p. 1212.

107Boyd. *op. cit.,* 81-119.

Imperialism Issues in Protection

The repeal of the Corn Laws in 1846, which made England a free trade nation, followed soon after the commercial class gained control of the nation's political power. Fifty years later this same class led the agitation for the overthrow of the very free trade principles which they had inaugurated earlier. In both instances the moving factor was the self-interest of those who constituted the commercial class. However, in the former case they coupled their self-interest with principles they believed to be universal and necessary for the common good of humanity. Adam Smith, Ricardo, the Mills, Cobden, Bright and the other followers of the Manchester School thought that their system, once adopted, would result in an increase in the general well-being of all peoples and in an easing of international tensions. Even though their dreams were never realized, free trade was responsible for the prosperity of Britain in the twenty-five or more years following the repeal of the Corn Laws. In that period England was truly the workshop of the world. The home of the industrial revolution, she enjoyed decided advantages in the manufacturing trade; there were no serious rivals until the last quarter of the nineteenth century brought the United States and Germany to the fore as British competitors.

In 1870 the foreign trade of Great Britain almost equalled the combined trade of France, Germany, and the United States. After that year, however, the trade of those three countries expanded enormously. In part this trend resulted from the discovery of the Gilchrest process for making steel from phosphorific iron ores of which Germany and the United States had large deposits, while England had little of it. The expanding manufacture of Germany and the United States resulted also from the expanding railways which enabled the necessary coal to be transported to the iron ore beds or *vice versa*. The extension of steel production increased the export of English coal, the shipments rising from 12 million tons in 1870 to 29 millions in 1889. With the exception of this export of coal, the major part of England's export trade was in cotton and woolen textiles and other manufactured goods;

in the same period, the chief exports of the United States were food-stuffs.

During this period, however, the weaknesses in British industry became apparent. That industry had been in operation for three or four generations; the resulting old plants in the factories and the dis-inclination of the British to hustle for new markets paved the way for the rise of foreign competition. German education in general, and par-ticularly in the chemical and electrical fields, was superior to that of England, a fact which resulted in Germany's taking the lead in those two industries. The English manufacturer made no attempt to satisfy the whims of his customers as did the Germans. While the English manufacturer insisted on shipping goods of a uniform character to all markets, his German competitor studied the varying desires of his customers and shipped accordingly. While the English manufacturer printed his catalogues almost exclusively in the English language, using the English system of weights and measures and the awkward price system of pounds, shillings, and pence, his German competitor printed catalogues in the languages of his customers, using their systems of weights and measures and their price systems. The German manu-facturer also studied the tariff schedules of the customer states to ad-vantage. If he found that tariffs were levied on the basis of gross weight, he shipped goods there in light packages, thus making a saving which he could pass on to the customer. The study of geography gave the Germans another advantage in their competition with Eng-land. The English manufacturer usually sent all goods intended for the United States to New York where they were transshipped to the interior by rail, the freight rates being somewhat high. The German, on the other hand, soon found that much could be saved in freight rates if he shipped his manufactured goods intended for the interior to ports on the Gulf coast where he could also take advantage of the Mississippi to lessen the freight cost. While English manufacturers tended to make expensive articles which they desired to sell in large quantities, their German competitors manufactured to meet the needs of less well-to-do consumers and, at the same time, were not averse to small orders. Thus the German tried to adapt his wares in accordance with his customers' desires while the English manufacturer continued in his static and unbending habits.

While the foreign trade of the English suffered at the hands of their competitors the depression of 1879-1882 crippled their home in-dustry. By 1887 trade was beginning to boom again, but from that depression British industry never really recovered. "Unemployed" and "unemployment" were first recorded in the *Oxford English Dictionary* in the years immediately following this crisis.

During this same period English agriculture suffered severe reverses. The railroad opened the vast prairies of the United States as farm land and the invention of reapers made extensive cultivation possible. This, coupled with the decline in the freight rates to Europe, flooded the grain markets of England and Continental Europe. In addition to this, the English farmers experienced a series of poor yields and a depression in meat and diary prices. The other European countries placed tariffs on imported foodstuffs in order to preserve their agricultural land, but England failed to do this. The English agricultural industry, which before 1880 had employed more workers than any other single British field, never recovered from the depression of the seventies, although the one that followed in the nineties was worse.

After 1880 the export of British goods such as textiles, woolens, linen, and steel declined sharply while the export of coal and machinery increased in response to the demands of the rising industrial countries. The decline of the former and the rise of the latter were due, in part, to the tariffs imposed by these countries. The former textile markets in Germany and the United States practically disappeared; certainly by 1900 the chief markets for English textiles were India and the East.[1] Seeing that trade continued to fall off while the trade of Germany and the United States, protected by tariffs, increased by leaps and bounds, the English manufacturer began to reason that tariffs caused prosperity. While they did not argue for a complete reversal of the principles of free trade, they demanded that the government at least impose retaliatory tariffs.

Also during that period, the commercial class revived the old mercantilist theory that colonies should be developed for the exclusive use and profit of the mother country. In a world in which tariffs were rising to exclude British goods, they argued that colonies were a necessity if Great Britain was to have an adequate supply of raw materials and a reasonably sufficient market within which to dispose of the resultant manufactured goods. Their idea that additional colonies would provide additional markets—the vain hope that trade followed the flag—was false, as an examination of the trade figures for that period indicates. Between 1883 and 1893 the annual trade of Great Britain decreased from 305,000,000 pounds to 277,000,000 pounds. During the same interval the British Empire expanded to include

Egypt, the Sudan, Nigeria, Somaliland, Bechuanaland, Zululand, East and Central Africa, Rhodesia, Upper Burma, and other territory—an addition of approximately four million square miles and a population of over one hundred million. But the colonies did not prove to be the valuable markets which Britain needed. This did not mean that there was no profit to be made in the colonies; Rhodes and his associates certainly made profitable investments there, as did many others; but an extension of the Empire did not prevent a marked reduction in Britain's total trade.

Further examination of the trade statistics for the latter portion of the nineteenth century indicates that Britain's trade with her colonies remained relatively stationary, while her trade with Russia, the United States, France, and Germany relatively increased. The colonies also tended to enlarge their trade with foreign countries, and their trade with Britain went down accordingly. Growth in the size of the Empire did not seem to benefit the total British trade, for as the Empire spread the Empire trade contracted, although foreign trade increased at the same time.[2]

These facts did not apparently alter the thinking of the commercial class of the period. They desired some reform in the fiscal policy of the Government toward imported goods, some change in the policy of free trade which their class had adopted in the previous generation. But they did not link this policy of reform with a philosophy of universal betterment as had been the case when the campaign for free trade was in progress. The agitation for tariff reform was exclusively one of self-interest; in the minds of the British industrialists it was probably a measure of self-preservation.

The proponents of tariff reform found their champion in the Colonial Secretary who, at Birmingham, had made a fortune in the screw trade of which he had an English monopoly. Chamberlain was a business man and was closely associated with the great industrialists in Birmingham; the Kenricks and the Nettlefords were his kinsmen; Jesse Collins was his closest friend. The interests of the Birmingham industrialists were his interests. Their economic plight undoubtedly influenced him in taking up his policy of tariff reform, but if his public statements be taken at face value, those economic interests played only a secondary role, for Chamberlain's chief concern was the unity of the Empire. Birmingham had formerly subscribed to the doctrines of Adam Smith and of Cobden and had rendered service to the whole of humanity, but in the last decade of the nineteenth century that industrial city put its faith in Protection. Joseph Chamberlain, a product of that city, had also been a defender of free trade and Liberal principles, but he too was converted to the idea of Protection although other influences worked to change his mind.

The depression of 1879 resulted in the rise of neo-Protectionism. By 1881 this movement was sufficiently strong to demand recognition in Parliament, for in that year C. T. Ritchie introduced a motion with the intention of placing the House of Commons on record as favoring tariffs. In speaking against this motion, Chamberlain contended that the depression was the result of other causes than Protection abroad. He pointed out that even during the depression the production of coal increased; he warned that the export of British goods would be irreparably harmed by the imposition of retaliatory duties, since such a move would cause the rest of the world to retaliate against British goods the more. He concluded his speech with a denunciation of food taxes; these words were to be quoted against him later:

> "Lastly, sir, is anyone bold enough to propose that we should put taxes upon food? . . . I can conceive it just possible, although it is very improbable, that under the sting of great suffering and deceived by misrepresentation the working classes might be willing to try strange remedies, and might be foolish enough to submit for a time to a proposal to tax the food of the country, but one thing I am certain of. If this course is ever taken, and if the depression were to continue, or to recur, it would be the signal for a state of things more dangerous and more disastrous than anything which has been seen in this country since the repeal of the Corn Laws."[3]

This was in line with Chamberlain's declaration that Britain's policy for many years had been favorable to the consuming interests of the community as a whole and not to the small producing interests of any particular section or class.[4] He was then of the opinion that there was no need to reverse the principles of free trade which had conferred immense benefits upon the industrial structure of Great Britain. Any tax on food would materially increase the living costs of the great majority of the working people while it would increase the profits of only a very small minority.[5]

While his public statements of this period indicated strong preference for the principles of free trade, in private he expressed opinions indicating that, as Lord Farrer, the head of the civil servants in the Board of Trade had said, he was not an orthodox free trader. In 1882 Britain renewed the trade treaty with France which Cobden had negotiated. At this time Chamberlain wanted to force a reduction of French duties by threatening to increase the English duties on French wines and favor those of Portugal, Spain, and Italy. He discussed the matter with his friend Dilke, who recorded in his diary:

"At this monment I called attention to the bearing of our most-favoured-nation clause treaties on the commercial condition of the British Empire generally, and pointed out that the bearing of the matter on the colonies would become very important some day; and I found even too much support from the Head of the Trade Department [Chamberlain], who was a Protectionist, or at least a strong Reciprocitarian, and who at once grasped my idea by arguing that there was a chance that there would be formed a British Zollverein, raising discriminatory duties upon foreign produce as against that of the British Empire."[6]

This was strangely prophetic of the stand Chamberlain was to take in future years.

In the election of 1885, the representatives from Birmingham for the first time contested single member districts. During this election Chamberlain found that whereas Birmingham had been considered "as Liberal as the sea is salt", there was strong Tory support in each of the divisions because of the hold that "fair trade" had on the artisans. Chamberlain spent much time in that campaign combating the evils of Protection, telling Russell that it required his utmost effort to win all the seats for the Liberal Party. Russell was of the opinion that this made a strong impression on Chamberlain and that it contributed largely to his later change of policy.[7]

In the campaign of that year Chamberlain continued his attacks on the evils that would result from a tax on food and the small loaf.[8] One of the Tory candidates advocated a tariff on timber to help the cabinet-makers. In reply Chamberlain said that Germany had done that very thing with the result that fewer cabinet-makers were employed and those that were worked longer hours and for less pay than before.[9] To those who argued that the depression was the result of the policy of free trade in Britain, Chamberlain replied that if that were true one ought to find a booming trade in those countries which had protective systems, but that in fact the depression effected the protected countries as it did Great Britain, and in his opinion the depression was worse in those countries than in England.[10] He was inclined to think that the fact that the United States and Germany had Protective systems caused those countries to buy more manufactured goods from England than they sent to that country. He argued that if they adopted free trade they would offer more serious competition to British industry than they did under their protected systems. In reply to the argument for retaliatory tariffs, he stated that such tariffs might be reasonable provided Great Britain could injure the trade of her foreign competitors without entailing any injury to herself, but that retaliation would surely invite like treatment from foreign countries which would be extremely harmful to British trade.[11]

With the passage of three short years, Chamberlain began to alter his opinions on tariffs and trade as he had done in other matters. As has been seen, he began to connect the expansion of Empire with the expansion of trade and to anticipate a scheme for Empire preference. In May, 1889, Colonel George T. Denison, who had long been a believer in such a policy, arrived from Canada and informed Chamberlain that the only hope for closer union lay in a system of reciprocal agreements which would give preference to English goods in colonial markets and to colonial goods in English markets. Chamberlain agreed to study the plan and to sponsor it if he found it feasible.[12] At this time, however, Chamberlain still believed that the Empire could be drawn together in a plan for mutual defense. All schemes of Empire defense turned finally on the ways and means of financing them, which naturally brought the commercial questions to the fore.

At the Colonial Conference of 1887 and again at the Ottawa Conference of 1894, proposals had been made to finance a joint plan of Imperial defense by imposing a two per cent duty on foreign goods, but no further action had been taken. No plan involving tariffs and a change in free trade principles received Chamberlain's support. However, he felt that the question of trade within the Empire deserved special study; soon after he became Colonial Secretary he sent out circulars to all the Colonial Governors asking for detailed surveys of trade. He desired not only trade statistics but also information about the displacement of British goods by foreign goods and the reasons therefor.[13] The undoubted purpose of this investigation was to stimulate inter-Imperial trade; possibly some form of Imperial Federation was at that time taking shape in Chamberlain's mind and he was looking for data in suport of his plan.

On March 25, 1896, Chamberlain outlined his first scheme for a commercial union of the Empire; he called it an Imperial Zollverein. Before giving the details of the scheme, Chamberlain reiterated his faith in free trade and his objection to the Protective system that would have been inaugurated by the proposal made at the Ottawa Conference. Under this plan Great Britain and the colonies would place no duties on the goods exchanged *inter alia*; each member would be allowed complete freedom in the arrangement of its tariff schedules applicable to foreign imports, but Great Britain would be required to levy a small duty on articles of widespread consumption which the colonies produced. These articles included corn, meat, wool, and sugar.[14] As German unity had been encouraged by the Zollverein, so might an Imperial Zollverein serve the same function in the unity of the Empire.

Chamberlain presented this plan as an extension of the principle of free trade, but certainly for England it was not an extension, for she would be forced to impose duties. Here also the plan seemed to run counter to Chamberlain's avowed objections to a tax on food. The similarity between the German Zollverein and the Imperial one he envisioned was not very great. The German Zollverein was an agreement between contiguous states; in such a situation the presence of tariff barriers impeded trade rather more than they would hamper trade between scattered countries. The members of the German Zollverein probably had more in common than did the various members of the British Empire for the simple reason that they were neighbors. The colonies far removed from the mother country had developed institutions, habits, and customs different from those of Great Britain. The wide extent and diversity of the Empire prevented any common tariff schedules, as Chamberlain himself realized when he proposed the scheme.

The plan which he proposed at the Canada Club dinner was not received well either at home or in the colonies. At home the suggestion of a change in the free trade policy of the country was naturally opposed by all Liberals and not a few Conservatives. In the colonies the tariffs had existed for a sufficient length of time to make their repeal practically impossible. The idea failed, but thoughts of unity still persisted in his mind. With the approach of the Queen's Jubilee Year, Chamberlain hoped that a Colonial Conference could be held to exchange views on the subject. The premiers from Canada, Newfoundland, New Zealand, Natal, the Cape Colony, and the six Australian colonies came to London for the Conference in June of 1897 as guests of the state. Prior to the assembling of the delegates Canada announced a preference of 12½% would be given to all British goods imported into Canada and that this preference would be increased to 25% the following year. This gave Chamberlain hope that some such scheme might be adopted by all the self-governing colonies.

The Colonial Conference which met from June 24 to July 8, 1897, was devoted to the exchange of ideas rather than to the formulation of any particular program. In discussing a possible Council of the

Empire, Sir Wilfred Laurier of Canada raised a question regarding the feasibility of the colonies' sending delegates to Westminster with the right to speak but not to vote, thus enabling the colonies to place their points of view before the public. No plans for a council of this sort came to fruition. In discussing Empire defense the colonies agreed to continue sending appropriations to support the naval and military forces, although Australia continued in her policy of maintaining squadrons for the defense of her home waters. Chamberlain talked of the possibility of an interchange of troops from time to time, with Great Britain sending detachments to the colonies and the colonies exchanging contingents and sending some troops to Great Britain. In discussing commercial relations, the colonial premiers indicated their disapproval of any Zollverein scheme, although they all indicated their support of the Canadian plan of giving preference to the goods of the mother country. They indicated that they would introduce the necessary legislation upon their return, but they could not guarantee the results.[15] From Chamberlain's point of view the Conference was hardly a success.

Although the Zollverein scheme seemed to be doomed, Chamberlain still referred to it in his public remarks. In his speeches the importance of commerce to the Empire assumed an increasing role. The Empire, he said, was commerce; as a Chamber of Commerce existed for the furtherance of trade just so Her Majesty's Government existed for the same purpose.[16] Statements such as these, when coupled with his declaration that Great Britain could not exist a day without the commerce of the Empire, are somewhat similar to certain Marxian ideas on imperialism. According to Marxist theory, the necessity for finding suitable areas of investment and the necessity of disposing of surplus goods led capitalist states inevitably to expand their control over backward areas. The difference between the Marxians and Chamberlain on this point is merely one of value judgment; the Marxians regarded such a policy as the bad fruit of a bad tree whereas Chamberlain considered it to be luscious fruit harvested from a diligently cultivated orchard. It is curious to note that in a speech in which he again referred to the worth of an Imperial Zollverein he attacked other nations for their tariff policies. He complained of the policy of other states which monopolized their colonial markets whereas Great Britain opened her colonies to the trade of the world. He stated that one of the reasons that compelled Britain to continue the expansion of her Empire was the fact that such a policy was necessary if free markets were to be maintained. If Britain had not taken what she could lay her hands on, the markets of the tropic regions would have been monopolized by other colonizing powers.[17] He neglected to state that the Zollverein would bring an end to these universal markets of which he was so proud and which, in his his estimation, resulted from the peculiar fitness of the British as a colonizing race.

In 1898 Chamberlain placed himself on record as opposed to countervailing duties because he thought they would be an infringement of the most-favored-nation clauses in the various trade treaties to which Britain was a party; such duties would interfere with trade and result in the disorganization of trade in general. He cited sugar as an example; in that commodity the duty would benefit only the 260,000 tons imported from the West Indies; since the total imports of sugar amounted to 1,500,00 tons the duty would not benefit that trade at all.[18] In June of 1899 he reversed his stand and spoke in favor of countervailing duties. These duties, intended to counteract the bounties of foreign governments, he declared, were not Protective and therefore not contrary to the principles of free trade.[19] Chamberlain was losing all his former scruples about the advisability of tariffs.

Heretofore he had had no opportunity to commit the Government to his views, but the necessity for finding revenue to meet the expenses of the South African War seemed to open the way. In May of 1902 the Cabinet decided to place a war tax of three pence per hundredweight on corn. Chamberlain defended this tax as a military necessity and then began to attack free trade as an antiquated system which had worked well at the time of its adoption, but was of no value under the changed conditions. Because of the rising hostility to Britain and the Empire in the international political world and because of the rising foreign tariffs, the Empire had to draw the ties of sentiment, sympathy, and interest more tightly together. To adhere to the shibboleth of free trade would be to pass up the one golden opportunity of closer union which the colonies had offered.[20]

Chamberlain hoped that the corn tax would prove to be an auspicious omen for the forthcoming Colonial Conference of June, 1902, which opened with much the same personnel as its predecessor of 1897, save that instead of six Australian premiers there was only one, for the Australian colonies had become federated in the meanwhile. In his opening address[21] the Colonial Secretary stated the three possible methods of unifying the Empire: in a political way through a Council of the Empire, in a military way through a league for defense, and in a commercial way through preferential tariffs. The colonies did not respond to the idea of political unity. Chamberlain had completely overlooked the growing feeling of separate nationality within each of the self-governing colonies. While the South African War may have shown the sentimental attachment of the colonies for the mother country, the military successes of the colonial troops had increased the impression of distinct nationhood held by the colonists. The colonies also turned deaf ears to the plea of Downing Street that England supported Imperial defense out of all proportion to its size and population. Canada declined to make any contribution whatsoever and the others made only nominal increases in their appropriations for this purpose. This left commercial measures as the only possible means of bringing the Empire into closer unity.

In addressing the Conference Chamberlain had indicated his support for a system of preferential tariffs, saying that the rising tariff barriers of the world had placed England in such a difficult position that she would be forced to impose tariffs in order to maintain her trade.[22] This seemed the only solution that the colonies would accept, as they had already indicated their disapproval of any Zollverein scheme of free trade with the Empire. The Colonial Conference passed a resolution recognizing

"that the principle of Preferential Trading between the United Kingdom and His Majesty's dominions beyond the seas would stimulate and facilitate mutual commercial intercourse, and would, by promoting the development of the resources and industries of the several parts, strengthen the Empire."[23]

With a view to implementing the spirit of this resolution, the Conference passed other resolutions calling on those colonies which had not already done so to give substantial preferential treatment to the products of the United Kingdom, and urging the Parliament at Westminster to grant preferential treatment to the products of the dominions when it imposed tariffs in the future.

After the meeting of the Colonial Conference, Canada added to the list of United Kingdom products which received a preferential treatment of 33⅓%; New Zealand granted a preferential treatment of 10% on manufactured articles; Cape Colony and Natal gave a preference of 25% to goods from the United Kingdom; Australia indicated that preference would be given but did not define what the terms would be.[24] The Cabinet did not take any action on the resolution; the leaders were still devoted to free trade. It appeared that Chamberlain could not count on any support for his scheme from the political leaders; he had the support of the colonies, which was of little assistance to him in forcing a change in British policy. His sole support in Britain came from those industries which hoped that tariffs would aid their respective products.

A few months after the meeting of the Colonial Conference Chamberlain departed for a tour of South Africa; there he assisted in the formation of a customs union between the four colonies in that area. Upon his return he found that C. T. Ritchie,[25] the new Chancellor of the Exchequer, had persuaded the Cabinet to repeal the corn duty imposed by Hicks-Beech. Ritchie had found that he would have a surplus in the treasury, thus making tax reductions possible. He argued that the repeal of the corn duty would relieve the indirect taxpayer; this argument might have been valid, but the corn duty had not resulted in a rise in the price of bread. The Cabinet agreed to the repeal because they feared that it might lead to further duties. This was what Chamberlain hoped for, but the Cabinet decision had robbed him of his entering wedge. He could not persuade the Cabinet to change its decision, and Ritchie introduced the budget on April 23, 1903.

Disappointed, Chamberlain resolved to appeal to the people on the tariff issue,[26] opening his campaign in Birmingham on May 15. Why did Chamberlain press this subject which was opposed by the Cabinet and the leaders of his Party? In the years since he had become Colonial Secretary he had become convinced that Imperial unity was the *sine que non* of the continued greatness of the Empire. He had sponsored the resolution passed by the Colonial Conference of 1902 which favored a preferential tariff; he probably felt responsible to the colonies for the success of the issue there raised. His desire to become Prime Minister perhaps played a part.[27] He had had this desire for some years. Had it not been for the split in the Liberal Party over the Irish Question he would, in all probability, have succeeded Gladstone as its leader. It had been said that he split with Gladstone on this issue in order to force the "Grand Old Man" out of office and take his place. This argument is hardly well-founded, however, as it is logical to assume that Chamberlain was experienced enough in politics to realize that his chances of becoming Prime Minister would have been greater had he supported Gladstone and placed himself in line for the succession when the Prime Minister retired. He gained nothing by forcing the issue. When Salisbury retired in July, 1902, Chamberlain might have hoped to succeed him. At the time of the Prime Minister's retirement Chamberlain was laid up as the result of a cab accident; Balfour succeeded to Salisbury's office without demur. Had Chamberlain not been incapacitated at the time, would he have been selected in Balfour's place? This was scarcely to be expected. He had not identified himself with the Conservatives until he took office in 1895 under Salisbury. Prior to that time he had called himself a Liberal Unionist, and he continued to refer to himself as a Unionist—even after 1895—and had sat opposite the Conservatives in the House of Commons. For this reason, even though he was the strongest man in Salisbury's Cabinet, he would have been unacceptable to the rank and file of the Conservative Party. In any case, with the selection of Balfour to succeed Salisbury, Chamberlain's chances of becoming Prime Minister declined. He might have reasoned that his only chance yet remaining to become the chief officer in His Majesty's Government was to succeed in some spectacular political *coup*. If he remained in the Cabinet, Balfour as Prime Minister would receive credit for any policy the Government might endorse. Therefore, his only hope lay in convincing the British public of the importance of some policy of his own contrivance which he could defend independently.

Chamberlain's program for tariff reform split the Cabinet; Balfour attempted in vain to heal the breach. On September 9 Chamberlain offered to resign in order to continue his efforts unhampered by Cabinet connections. Balfour did not act on his resignation but on September 14, dismissed C. T. Ritchie and Lord Balfour of Burleigh, the most ardent champions of free trade. The next day Lord George Hamilton anl the Duke of Devonshire resigned, although Balfour persuaded the Duke to remain, but on the following day Balfour announced the acceptance of Chamberlain's resignation. Both Chamberlain and the free traders felt that Balfour had deceived them as he had not informed either that his opponent was leaving the Cabinet. Soon afterward the Duke of Devonshire resigned the second time; this time the resignation was accepted. In reconstructing his Cabinet, Balfour made Austen Chamberlain Chancellor of the Exchequer and appointed Victor Cavendish, a nephew of the Duke, Financial Secretary of the Treasury, thus keeping open channels of communication with the tariff reformers and free traders. On September 20, Balfour enunciated his own program, intended as a compromise solution of the differences which had split the Cabinet. Without declaring for a general tariff or a tax on food, he spoke in favor of attempting to force foreign governments to reduce their tariffs on British goods through the use of retaliatory tariffs. This program offended the orthodox free traders and did not please Chamberlain since it offered no hope for a preferential system functioning in co-operation with the Dominions—an essential element in his scheme for the unity of the Empire. But we are getting ahead of the story; let us return to the opening of Chamberlain's campaign and his arguments for tariff reform.

After his speech on May 15, Chamberlain did not press the campaign for tariff reform until after his resignation from the Cabinet. Then he organized a Tariff Reform League to collect a war-chest and to disseminate information. Professor W. A. S. Hewins became the economic advisor of the organization. Chamberlain travelled the length and breadth of England preaching his new gospel with all the fervor of an evangelist. What was his argument?

Chamberlain was careful to make the break with free trade seem less drastic than it really was. He said that he did not believe in being bound by any technical definition of free trade; his chief object was to seek free exchange of goods with all the countries of the world, but to make this possible it was necessary that Britain regain her freedom and the power of negotiation through the imposition of tariffs.[28] In his opinion a scheme of preferential tariffs was the only method of bringing the colonies into a union with Britain. He had tried to interest the colonies in a Council of the Empire and in a Defense League, but they had not been receptive. They supported preferential tariffs, however; a commercial union based on preferential tariffs would necessitate a Council of Empire which would make for "a great, united, loyal, and federated Empire."[29] Chamberlain was convinced that the future greatness of the Empire depended upon the success of this commercial union which he fostered.[30] His main purpose in agitating for tariff reform was to increase the solidarity of the Empire; fiscal reform was secondary to this purpose.[31]

At Glasgow on October 6, Chamberlain declared that he had two purposes in launching his tariff reform. The first was to increase the strength and prosperity of the United Kingdom, enabling her to continue to play a great role in world history. His second object was

"the realisation of the greatest ideal which has ever inspired statesmen in any country or in any age—the creation of an Empire such as the world has never seen. We have to cement the union of the states beyond the seas; we have to consolidate the British race; we have to meet the clash of competition, commercial now—sometime in the past it has been otherwise—it may be again in the future. Whatever it be, whatever danger threatens, we have to meet it no longer as an isolated country; we have to meet it fortified and strengthened and buttressed by all those of our kinsmen, all those powerful and continually rising states which speak our common tongue and glory in our common flag."[32]

Chamberlain went about as a missionary of Empire, urging a change in old ideas in order to prevent the disintegration of the Empire and to prevent the loss of "the results of centuries of noble effort and patriotic endeavor."[33] He appealed to the British public in the name of the eleven million colonists who were British in race, religion, and traditions and who wanted to unite the Empire by means of a commercial union.[34] To refuse to co-operate with the Dominions would mean that an opportunity for preserving the Empire would be lost—perhaps never to return again.[35] He declared that he was concerned only incidentally about making Britain richer; his main endeavor was to insure the future greatness of the widespread Empire;[36] it so happened, he said, that his policy would also increase the material welfare of the people of Britain.[37]

Chamberlain desired a commercial union not because he doubted the loyalty of the colonies to the Empire and wanted to erase that doubt by forming the union, but he wanted the union in order to make the loyalty of the colonies effective. Without unity each Dominion was forced to act individually to meet the threats to its trade; under a unified system the strength of the whole Empire could be organized to meet such threats. Such a union would also pave the way for unified action in time of war if that ever became necessary.[38]

Chamberlain contended, contrary to facts shown by the trade statistics, that the colonies were the best customers of Great Britain. Therefore, a refusal to adopt a plan sponsored by the colonies would result in heavy losses, unemployment, and lowered wages.[39] The Imperial trade was in his estimation essential to the prosperity of the United Kingdom. If that trade were to decline Great Britain would sink immediately in rank and become possibly a fifth-rate power.[40] Since trade had created the British Empire and stimulated the best qualities of the British race,[41] Britain ought to do all in its power to preserve that trade. Under an efficiently organized and managed system the British Empire might become entirely self-sufficient, since all the necessities and luxuries of life could be produced somewhere within the vast domain of the Empire.[42]

In presenting his case for tariff reform, Chamberlain stated that Britain's trade with the colonies in the past twenty or thirty years had remained stationary while the trade with the protected countries had decreased. A preferential tariff would increase the trade with the colonies, but it would not harm the trade with the protected countries which was decreasing in any event.[43] In actual fact, Britain's trade with the protected countries had declined in certain commodities—wool, linen, and other textiles, but the trade in steel, machinery, and coal had increased enormously. Chamberlain emphasized the fact that there had been an increase in colonial trade in 1902 and stated that this increase could be enhanced by adopting his plan.[44] It is generally held, however, even by those who wrote contemporaneously, that 1902 was an abnormal year and that the increase in colonial trade then resulted from the Boer War. The Little Englanders argued that, since Britain's trade with the colonies was less than that with foreign countries, the British people ought to seek to increase the trade with the foreign countries, which were better customers. On Chamberlain, seeking Empire unity, this argument made no impression. In order to increase the colonial trade he was willing to decrease the foreign trade.[45] Some sacrifices had to be made for the sake of the Dominions, for the Dominions were practically independent states which would drift away if no efforts were made to hold them within the Empire.[46]

While sacrifices should be made, Chamberlain seemed to think that even if tariffs were imposed on foreign goods, the foreign country would absorb the duty so that the British would not be called upon to sacrifice anything. Professor A. C. Pigou wrote a letter to *The Times*[47] contesting this point of view. The amount of the duty assumed depended in a large part on the nature of the demand for the taxed commodity. If the demand was great the purchaser would be forced to assume the duty. In those cases where the demand was negligible and the amount of money spent for the taxed article could easily be shifted to other purchases, the foreigner would assume the duty in a large part.

Chamberlain contended that since the prosperity of the protected countries had increased to a greater extent and more rapidly than had that of Britain, a Protective system would enable Britain to increase her prosperity.[48] This argument Pigou also attacked by saying that many factors other than the tariff entered into the reasons for the prosperity of the protected countries which, in his estimation, had not increased with greater rapidity than that of Britain.

Under Chamberlain's scheme, Britain would levy a duty of two shillings per quarter on foreign corn, 5% on foreign meat and dairy products exclusive of bacon. On the other hand, his plan provided for a reduction of the duty on tea, sugar, coffee, and cocoa.[49] Since corn, meat, and dairy products were the chief products of the colonies, duties on foreign imports of these commodities were necessary in order to enable the colonies to sell in the British market.[50] By taking the tax off tea, sugar, and cocoa, Chamberlain hoped to stimulate greater consumption of these articles. The tax lost in this instance would be regained by taxing other food products, corn, meat, and dairy products.[51] Under such a scheme, Chamberlain declared, the cost of food would not increase; he hoped that the artisan and the agricultural laborer would save at least half a farthing[52] each week as a result.[53] He made his appeal to the working men on these grounds.[54]

Chamberlain confessed that his experiences in the Colonial Office had altered his views on free trade:

"I was brought up myself in the true orthodoxy of Free Trade, and, even after I had come to have doubts on the subject, I do not think that I should have made myself a protagonist in this struggle if it had not been for my experiences in that great office which I recently filled; had it not been for the knowledge I gained there, and from what I learned of the opinion of our kinsmen across the seas, and the impression which was made upon me that this Empire, to the continuous existence of which I attach such deep and tremendous importance, could not permanently be kept together without some strengthening of the bonds which, at present, bind us one to the other. . . . Our great Imperial principle is to treat each other better than we are treated by any one else."[55]

His experiences at the Colonial Office having convinced him that the Empire should be strengthened, Chamberlain had adopted that scheme which he thought most likely to do this even though that plan went contrary to the principles of free trade, which

"was an anti-Imperial policy. . . . Is it not fair, is it not reasonable, that those of us who thought our Imperialism was quite consistent with Free Trade should now review our position when we find the leaders of Free Trade not only contemplating the possibility of this disruption of the Empire, but declaring as their private conviction, hope, and aspiration that the policy of Free Trade would lead indirectly, but certainly, to this result?"[56]

In this connection Balfour wrote:

"Joe was becoming an Imperialist, and he saw that Imperialism was impossible on the bare naked Free Trade basis—or at any rate that it would lose half its strength."[57]

This stand of Chamberlain's was in agreement with Hobson's argument that an Imperialist was an open and avowed Protectionist.[58] Hobson, writing in 1901, had prophesied the coming of Chamberlain's program of Tariff Reform. He said:

"Protection will not be Protection, but Free Trade within the Empire; a protectionist tariff will hide its exclusive side and masquerade as an Imperial Zollverein. Great economic changes, requiring the use of political machinery, invent that machinery. The Imperialism of England, essentially though not exclusively an economic thing, will strive to cover the protective system of finance it favours, by a great political achievement, entitled Federation Within the Empire.

This avenue to Protection would in any case have been essayed by Imperialism, as indeed the curious attempt of Mr. Chamberlain in 1897 testifies. The abnormal swelling of financial needs due to the disastrous policy in South Africa merely precipitates this policy and gives it political occasion. It will be sought to exploit the enthusiastic loyalty of the colonists exhibited in their rally around the mother country in the South African War for purposes of formal federation on a basis which shall bind them to contribute money and men to the protection of the Empire."[59]

Whatever may have been Chamberlain's purpose in launching his scheme for tariff reform his plan did not elicit the response for which he had hoped. His tariff reform for the sake of the unity of the Empire degenerated into Tariff Reform for the revival of this or that sick industry, as the titles of his later speeches indicate. At the opening of his campaign he had described the tariff duties which would be imposed as only incidentally Protective[60] since Empire unity was his goal, but he did not stress this point in the latter stages of his fight.

While Chamberlain's tariff reform scheme caused a rift in the ranks of the Conservatives, it served to solidify the Liberals who were drawn together to combat the threat to free trade. Balfour attempted to reform his shattered forces; in January, 1905, he announced a plan for retaliatory duties and duties for purposes of negotiations as a compromise plan. The fact that the Chamberlainites delayed two months before accepting his plan indicated the futility of the attempted reunion. Balfour could not count on Chamberlain's backing in the event of a vote on fiscal reform; when the opposition forced a vote on this subject Balfour persuaded his followers to abstain from voting, which convinced the public that he had been in office too long. He resigned in December of 1905, Campbell-Bannerman and the Liberals taking over. At the election which followed in January the Conservatives saved only 157 seats, Balfour himself being defeated.

This public disapproval of Chamberlain's policy, so striking in its nature, marked the end of the tariff reform scheme. It also proved to be the last act in Chamberlain's public career, as he suffered a paralytic stroke in July of 1906 which ended his public life. The invalid lived in retirement until his death in July, 1914.

Chamberlain had completely changed his views on tariffs in this period of his career. He began as a believer in free trade, opposed to retaliatory and countervailing duties. But the development of his Imperial ideas led him to the conclusion that the closer unity of the Empire was necessary for its continued greatness. He became willing to change any of his views which stood in the way of the realization of this "great dream." The first modification came when he proposed an Imperial Zollverein; from there he progressed by logical stages to a defense of retaliatory and countervailing duties, and finally to a well-developed scheme of protective duties on food and other commodities.

It has already been noted that after Chamberlain became an Imperialist as the result of his split with Gladstone over Irish Home Rule in 1886, he had subordinated all other considerations to the paramount concern of his later political career—imperialism. Chamberlain's repudiation of free trade and his acceptance of Protection was but another piece of evidence which indicated that imperialism was the primary concern of his life.

REFERENCES

[1]*Cf.* C. K. Ensor, *England, 1870-1914* (Oxford, 1936), Chs. IV and IX for details.
[2]*Cf.* Hobson, *op. cit.,* 27-32; Berard, *op. cit.,* 89 ff.
[3]Boyd, *op. cit.,* I, 103.
[4]*Hansard,* Fourth Series, v. 115, p. 272.
[5]*Ibid.,* 273.
[6]Gwynn and Tuckwell, *op. cit.,* I, 401.
[7]G. W. E. Russell, "Joseph Chamberlain," *Contemporary Review,* v. 37, n. s. 317.
[8]Boyd, *op. cit.,* 175-76.
[9]*The Times,* November 10, 1885.
[10]*Ibid.,* November 11, 1885.
[11]*Ibid.,* November 13, 1885.
[12]Garvin, *op. cit.,* II, 468-69.
[13]Cmd., 8449, 1897.
[14]*For. & Col. Speeches, op. cit.,* 98.
[15]Garvin, *op. cit.,* II, 185-192.
[16]*The Times,* January 19, 1898.
[17]*Ibid.*
[18]*Ibid.*
[19]*Hansard,* Fourth Series, v. 72, p. 1296.
[20]*The Times,* May 17, 1902.
[21]Cmd., 1299, 1902.
[22]*Ibid.,* 9.
[23]C. A. Vince, *Mr. Chamberlain's Proposals* (London, 1903), 7.
[24]L. Creswicke, *The Life of J. Chamberlain* (London, 1904-5), III, 175-80.
[25]It will be remembered that in 1881 C. T. Ritchie had introduced a motion in Parliament favoring fair trade. He, too, had reversed his stand.
[26]Garvin's biography of Chamberlain is complete only to 1900; there is, therefore, no record of his private correspondence available for this period.
[27]*Cf.* T. W. Mitchell, "The Development of Chamberlain's Fiscal Policy," *Ann. Am. Acad. Pol. & Soc. Sci.,* no. 405, p. 119.
[28]Boyd, *op. cit.,* II, 139.
[29]*Ibid.,* 186.
[30]*The Times,* June 15, 1903.
[31]Vince, *op. cit.,* 1; Archibald McGoun, *The Revenue Tariff Within the Empire,* (Montreal, 1904), 38.
[32]Boyd, *op. cit.,* 143.
[33]*Ibid.,* 164.

³⁴*Tariff Reform Speeches, op. cit.*, 99.
³⁵*Ibid.*, 188.
³⁶*Ibid.*, 204.
³⁷*The Times*, January 12, 1904.
³⁸Boyd, *op. cit.*, 273-4; 306; 326.
³⁹*Ibid.*, 299; 185.
⁴⁰*Ibid.*, 148; *The Times*, January 5, 1906.
⁴¹*Ibid.*, May 9, 1906.
⁴²Boyd, *op. cit.*, 153.
⁴³*Tariff Reform Speeches, op. cit.*, 124.
⁴⁴*Ibid.*, 126.
⁴⁵Boyd, *op. cit.*, 131.
⁴⁶*The Times*, June 5, 1905; *Tariff Reform Speeches, op. cit.*, 160-61; Boyd, *op. cit.*, 296.
⁴⁷May 16, 1904.
⁴⁸*Tariff Reform Speeches, op. cit.*, 125. He had expressed the opposite view in 1885, as previously indicated.
⁴⁹Boyd, *op. cit.*, 158-59.
⁵⁰*The Times*, June 8, 1903.
⁵¹*Hansard*, Fourth Series, v. 147, p. 1017.
⁵²A farthing is one-fourth of an English penny.
⁵³*Tariff Reform Speeches, op. cit.*, 129.
⁵⁴*Ibid.*, 98.
⁵⁵Boyd, *op. cit.*, 256.
⁵⁶*Tariff Reform Speeches, op. cit.*, 173-4.
⁵⁷B. E. C. Dugdale, *Arthur James Balfour* (London, 1936), I, 345.
⁵⁸Hobson, *op. cit.*, 60.
⁵⁹*Ibid.*, 93.
⁶⁰*Hansard*, Fourth Series, v. 123, p. 187.

The Basis of the New Imperialism

It has already been noted that Chamberlain's ideas concerning the superiority of the British as a race and their mission were quite similar to other Imperialists of his day. He probably began to think along these lines under the influence of his friend Charles Dilke. Returning from a trip around the world, Dilke had written of the racial pride which was to become the dominant note in British political thinking of the future:

"In 1866 and 1867, I followed England round the world: everywhere I was in English-speaking or in English-governed lands. If I remarked that climate, soil, manners of life, that mixture with other peoples, had modified the blood, I saw, too, that in essentials the race was always one. The idea which in all the length of my travels has been my fellow and my guide—a key wherewith to unlock the hidden things of strange new lands—is a conception, however imperfect, of the grandeur of our race, already girdling the earth, which it is destined, perhaps eventually, to overspread."[1]

Race was to Dilke the primary consideration in political philosophy. He surveyed the world and imagined that the Anglo-Saxon race was the only one which could maintain its freedom. He spoke disparagingly of the French, the Swiss, the Russians, and the Spaniards; however, he looked with favor upon "our Teuton brethren."[2] Regarding the colonizing activities of the British, Dilke thought there was no need to suffer any qualms of conscience. The backward races had no sentiment of nationality and their anarchial systems were obstacles to progress. To him the worst exercise of political power by the Anglo-Saxon race was preferable to the best native administration.[3]

Writing in 1867 of the self-governing colonies, Dilke felt that so long as these colonies wished to be joined to England they should remain an integral part of the Empire, but that England would be benefited by their separation. The destiny of the race loomed so large in Dilke's thought that it did not seem important to him that Canada, Australia, and other self-governing colonies should remain integral parts of the Empire. So long as "Alfred's laws and Chaucer's tongue are theirs," he thought the triumph of any portion of the race was indicative of the good qualities inherent in the whole race.[4] Size was not, for Dilke, a criterion of prestige; this fact contributed to his indifference to the retention of the self-governing colonies. The passage of time resulted in a change in his views; in 1890, when his *Problems of Greater Britain* appeared, the desirability of the unity of the Empire was a fundamental premise.[5]

Dilke did not think that the continued unity of the Empire, as expressed through stronger ties between Great Britain and the Dominions, would benefit British trade. However, he did think that large amounts of British capital had been invested there at lower rates than would have been possible had the colonies been held by other states. He also desired the unity of the Empire because he felt that "the widening of the moral and intellectual horizons by the world-wide character of the British Empire [was] of equal advantage to the home-staying Briton."[6] Dilke, however, saw what Chamberlain had not seen; he perceived that the rising tide of colonial nationalism stood as an obstacle to all plans for Empire unity.[7]

The ideas which appeared in Dilke's writings probably influenced Chamberlain's thinking in a large measure; his ideas on the racial superiority of the British might have originated there, but at the time when he gave them their fullest expression they were a part of the *lingua franca* of British thought. The moral fervor and emotional force of the English, which had found an outlet in religion prior to the decline in faith which followed in part from the writings of Charles Darwin, now had to seek new channels. The British found this necessary substitute in nationalism and imperialism. Their interest and activity in this direction were given scientific justification by Walter Bagehot in his *Physics and Politics*, published in 1872.

Bagehot's study of evolution convinced him that human equality was a myth and that no such thing as natural law existed. Humanity and the individual did not loom large in the evolutionary process; in history the individual was always found in groups, each group having its own peculiar characteristics. The struggle for existence motivated the activities of these socio-political groups in their dealings one with the other. Bagehot found in the interplay of these groups a scientific basis for the identity of right and might:

"In every particular state of the world, those nations which are strongest tend to prevail over the others, and in certain marked peculiarities the strongest tend to be the best."[8]

Since the appearance of man upon the earth few nations had been able to climb from tribal organizations to fully developed states. Of those few, England excelled all others in the moderation, the balance of mind, and the energy which were so necessary to this exaltation. Only fully developed states were capable of having colonies; since England was the most advanced, the best, and the strongest of the existing states, she was most capable of administering these colonies.[9]

While Bagehot was among the first to interweave the theories of Darwin with the social progress of human beings, the case for social evolution received a more extended and a more cogent discussion in the works of Benjamin Kidd. His book, *Social Evolution,* published in 1894, sold over 250,000 copies within the next six years. Kidd pressed evolution into the service of imperialism and supplied the chief moral support for its doctrines.[10] "Progress," he stated, "everywhere from the beginning of life has been effected in the same way, and it is possible in no other. It is the result of selection and rejection."[11] Evolution from tribal organization to the modern state was not primarily intellectual in Kidd's estimation. After man became a social creature he ceased to develop his intellect and subordinated the rational desires of the individual to the widening needs of the group. The race which was the most socially efficient rather than the one which was most intellectual achieved primacy among the races. The characteristics which made a race socially efficient were "a pure domestic life, honesty, courage, uprightness, good judgment." All these characteristics were possessed by the Anglo-Saxon people who were, therefore, the most socially efficient race. These characteristics had been developed because of the religious and humanitarian views of the Anglo-Saxons rather than because of any intellectual superiority.

If one race was more socially efficient than another in any marked degree, the superior race ought to administer the affairs of the inferior. By pointing to the undeveloped possibilities of Haiti, the West Indies, Central and South America, Kidd demonstrated that the tropical races were socially inefficient. Since the races living in the temperate zones were more socially efficient they ought to control the tropical regions for the general welfare of humanity. Kidd felt that the Anglo-Saxons had indicated through their administration of India and Egypt that, of the races within the temperate zone, they were the most fit to control tropical regions. This control was necessary not only for humanitarian reasons, but also for the added reasons that the tropics were a potential source of the future food supply of Europe. The spirit of altruism and social responsibility developed by the British since the days of the Reformation was a guarantee that their control would be in the interests of the general welfare rather than for the purposes of human exploitation. Even those humanitarian motives could not arrest an irrestible destiny, for the Anglo-Saxons, Kidd pointed out, had exterminated the less-developed races even more effectively than had other Europeans. Since Kidd wanted to administer the tropical colonies from the temperate zones with a minimum of white officials, the tropics not being the natural habitat of the white man, he did not want the policy of extermination to continue. The natives would furnish the necessary labor supply.[12]

Another writer in the same vein was Professor Karl Pearson who added to the scientific creed of imperialism.[13] He argued that the law of struggle in the lower forms of life was sufficient for the whole of sociology. Within the national group the struggle might be suspended to a certain extent, but to attain a high degree of development the struggle had to be maintained between the various national groups; the group that was the more mentally and physically fit would survive.[14]

Expansion of Empire was "in the air," so to speak. Chamberlain's views were not novel. They merely expressed the *milieu* of the age. It has already been indicated that his views on the peculiar fitness of the British to undertake the civilizing mission set before her were similar to those of Milner, Rhodes, Curzon, and Rosebery. Chamberlain could also find support for his belief that the size of the Empire was a good in itself in the general thought pattern of the day. In support of this view, and also in support of his plan for the closer unity of the Empire, he had but to turn to Professor Seeley's *Expansion of England*, which appeared in 1883.

Seeley was not an advocate of imperialism if by that term is meant a desire for the expansion of the Empire. He thought that the Empire grew without plan "in a fit of absence of mind"; the accidental course of European diplomacy had enabled Britain to retain control of this haphazardly acquired estate. But the Empire so gained offered a great opportunity to Britain. The future history lay in the hands of the great states, but Britain would not be as influential as it might be in the councils of Europe until it ceased to regard itself as a mere island kingdom. To prevent Russia or the United States from becoming more powerful than Britain, the British people had to be made to feel that Australia was as much a part of Britain as was Dorsetshire.[15] Seeley did not work out a plan by which this could be accomplished, and he seemed to have overlooked, as Chamberlain and so many of his contemporaries did, the rising nationalism in the Dominions, nurtured in part by the difficulties of transportation and communication which were not present in a country of great land mass as the United States. Seeley's argument for a more substantial connection between the colonies and the United Kingdom was a great aid to Chamberlain in popularizing his idea for a preferential tariff agreement.

While the intellectuals were writing learned treatises which tended to make imperialism "the latest philosophy of history and almost the last dogma of religion,"[16] the rise of the sensational press made easy the spread of this doctrine among those who had learned to read without having learned what to read. The motto of *The Daily Mail*, a representative paper, was "Empire first, and parish afterward." *The Daily Mail* conceived itself to be the spokesman of the Imperial idea. To use a phrase which would have been easily understood by the readers of this newspaper, it was a "tub-thumper" for the spread of British domination which was supposed to mean protection for the weak, and justice and liberty for the oppressed and the downtrodden. Even the staid old *Times* did not differ from the sensational press save in the quality of its verse, its style, its price, and the grade of its paper. In both *The Times* and *The Daily Mail* one found contempt for moral ideals and confidence in the efficacy of force.[17]

The popularity of imperialism at this time was due in a large measure to the reception given to Rudyard Kipling, the poet of imperialism. Although critics may question the quality of his poetry, none can question the fact that it was immensely popular and that it helped make imperialism not only acceptable but also respectable. Kipling spoke of the British as a people "absolute, strong, and wise" who were entitled to take anything that their hearts desired. It was he who coined the phrase "White Man's Burden" to dignify the policy of imperialism. Those who were anti-imperialistic attacked his support of British imperialism as "pious cant" and spoke of Kipling as "the poet of the barrack-room cad."[18]

The ideas expressed by Chamberlain, it has been seen, were but an indication of the trend in the thinking of the British people. But this trend was not confined to the British alone; a similar trend appeared simultaneously in Europe, America, and Asia. Historian John Fiske was the chief apostle of social Darwinism in the United States. He believed that the institutions of the Anglo-Saxons were superior to all others; because of this superiority that race would grow in power and in numbers until the whole earth became English in habits, language, political institutions, and religion. Josiah Strong, a Congregational clergyman of the same period, also had great faith in the Anglo-Saxon race which had contributed more to the development of two great ideals than any other race. These two ideals were civil liberty and a pure spiritual Christianity; because these two ideals were so well developed among Anglo-Saxons, Strong declared that they had been divinely commanded to be their brothers' keeper. God was training the Anglo-Saxons for the final competition of the races. The chosen race would triumph and would spread over Mexico, Central and South America, the islands of the sea, and Africa. The other races would be conquered, subdued and "Anglo-Saxonized."

Yet another believer in the superiority of one race over others was Professor John W. Burgess. The race which Burgess thought to be superior was the Teutonic—of which the Anglo-Saxon was a branch. Burgess, while doing advanced work in various German universities, studied the various races and found the Greeks, the Slavs, the Celts, and the Romans all inferior to the Teutons who had created the national state which was, in his opinion, "the most modern and most complete solution of the problem of political organization which the world has as yet produced." Because of this they were entitled to be the leaders in the organization and administration of states and were entrusted with the mission of "conducting the political civilization of the modern world." Particularly was this true with reference to the backward races. The barbarians had no right to remain barbaric; the Teutonic peoples ought to aid and direct their civilization. If opposition to this civilizing mission developed, the Teutons were not only obliged but in duty bound to force civilization upon the barbarians. Someone has said that Burgess did not send the Teutonic state on its mission with the Biblical slogan of "the sword of the Lord and of Gideon," but that he accomplished the same purpose by sending it out under the aegis of "world-duty."[19]

It was during this period that the United States annexed Hawaii, took the Philippines and Puerto Rico from Spain, and began the systematic penetration of the Caribbean area. On the continent of Europe the idea of the superiority of the Teutonic race—which Burgess had so thoroughly absorbed—contributed to the reasons for Germany's policy of colonial expansion. In the Far East Japan was beginning her career of imperialism with a war against China. The Japanese easily built support for their program of expansion from their religious traditions which made them a chosen people with a divine mission to "Japanize" the East if not the entire world.

In England itself very few writers appeared to contest the view that the British were a superior race particularly fitted to colonize and civilize the world. At the turn of the century J. A. Hobson and L. T. Hobhouse began to oppose the contentions of Kidd, Pearson, and others who had similar ideas. Their writings came too late to have any influence on Chamberlain's policy. Hobson denied that progress was possible only through a struggle between races in which the strongest survived. He was not averse to the use of the term struggle itself, but he thought that it could be interpreted in a manner other than that used by the biological sociologists. He spoke of the higher struggle of man in the realm of intellectual ideas—a struggle to advance the general welfare of all humanity—as a type of struggle which would bring out the finest and best in all races. He did not believe that the national state was the ultimate form of political organization or that strife between nation-states was absolutely necessary. He persisted in the old idea of the nineteenth-century liberals that the nation was but one stage in the development of political organization.[20]

Three years after Hobson's *Imperialism* appeared, Hobhouse wrote his *Democracy and Reaction*. In this work he discussed the intellectual reaction against the principles of Liberalism. He believed that one of the reasons for the popularity of the views of Kidd, Pearson, and other social Darwinians was that the middle class had become satisfied and complacent. That class had championed reforms only until it had received certain privileges through the limited extension of those reforms. It then forgot the universal application of the principles upon which it had demanded reform. Being satisfied, it yielded to the grandiose imperial schemes which appealed to its vanity. Hobhouse discussed the falsity of the views on race struggle and redefined the function of reason—neglected or ignored by Kidd and the others—in society in terms of correlation and adjustment. He retained his faith in the ultimate triumph of rationalism, believing that once the falsities of the views on social evolution were made apparent they would cease to exist. In place of a policy of imperialism the people would support a program leading to the eventual coalescence of Liberalism and Socialism.[21]

Although the intellectual current of the times offered an adequate background for Chamberlain's imperialism, it would be unfair to say that Chamberlain was a mere pawn in the irresistible movement of history. Without his driving energy imperialism would not have been as vigorous as it was in the latter years of the nineteenth century. Robertson has said:

"What lies especially at his door [Chamberlain's] is the responsibility for the sins of the new movement of vulgar and vicious 'Imperialism,' which dates broadly from the time of his appearance as a Tory minister."[22]

Chamberlain's son, Austen, also indicated that he thought his father was responsible for the "New Imperialism," but to him the movement was a virtuous one. In his opinion his father "breathed a new spirit into the Empire, and changed the course of our Imperial development."[23]

In reality, of course, the elder Chamberlain had only fallen heir to the policy of Disraeli, expanding and broadening it. Disraeli espoused a policy of imperialism for several reasons, partly as a policy suitable for gaining votes, more as a belief in the extension of Empire as a value in itself. He also wanted to consolidate the existing Empire in order to strengthen the position of England in world affairs. In 1867 Disraeli defined his policy as one of *Imperium et Libertas*. He paid more attention to the former than to the latter. He was much more interested in ruling than in granting liberty and freedom. The same might be said of Chamberlain. One cannot review his earlier career without being convinced that he had, as Disraeli claimed he himself had, a great passion for the welfare of the exploited masses, but he did not have an equal concern for liberty and freedom. Gladstone once referred to Chamberlain as *"un homme autoritaire";* others have noted his "love of governance, of domination, of having his own way."[24] He was given to an admiration of administrative strength and efficiency rather than to a concern for the liberty of the people.

Disraeli and Chamberlain were not aristocratic by birth. Disraeli always had a deep admiration for the aristocracy and looked upon it as the balance wheel in the struggle between the middle class and the exploited workers. Despite the fact that he was frowned upon by the aristocrats, he succeeded in moving in their circles and in adopting their philosophy in general. Chamberlain had, in his early days, a deep and abiding contempt for the aristocracy. Yet, not long after he made his most biting attack upon the aristocrats in the person of Lord Salisbury, he was co-operating with them in a successful effort to defeat the Home Rule Bill. From that time forward he began to associate himself with aristocrats and to espouse aristocratic principles, although the aristocrats looked askance at him as they had at Disraeli.

Since both Disraeli and Chamberlain adopted an aristocratic out-look did their imperialism derive from that outlook? Joseph Schumpeter has suggested that imperialism is a policy peculiar to aristocracies.[25] Imperialism, he argued, is a product of feudal society and has no place in a capitalistic order. The fundamental basis of feudalism was land power—the more land a feudal lord held the more power he had. Feudal society was characterized by wars between feudal lords intent on extending their power. A desire for larger and larger landed estates thus became inherent in the thinking of the feudal aristocrats. With the decline of feudalism and the development of capitalism, this land-hunger should have disappeared, for capitalism is based on free com-petitive exchange in which there is no place for force and violence. However, in the change from feudalism to capitalism, the feudal aristocracy, or more properly their descendants, continued in places of power in the government of their respective states. This was especially true within the foreign offices. Since the landed aristocrats, with the disappearance of feudalism, were no longer able to satisfy their desire to gain control over more land in their own communities, they turned that desire into a policy of acquiring control over land in other parts of the world on behalf of the state. Imperialism thus resulted from an atavistic desire for an extended landed estate. Schumpeter believed that when the bourgeoisie gained complete control of the government and when the influence of the aristocracy disappeared imperialism would naturally decline, since there would be no basis for it.

When Chamberlain identified himself with the aristocracy the identification was, in all probability, only superficial. It is doubtful that he would have been able to adopt completely all the traditions of the aristocracy; nor is it likely that he could have grafted upon himself this supposedly atavistic passion of the aristocracy for more land. Whatever may have been his social desires, Chamberlain was a product of mid-dle-class environment, not an aristocratic one. He probably was in-fluenced a great deal by those of his associates who were members of the aristocracy, but his policies were not wholly determined as a result of this association. As far as Chamberlain is concerned, it does not seem that Schumpeter's theory is applicable. It is unlikely, also, that this theory is applicable to the total movement of imperialism in this period. Disraeli and Rhodes were not aristocrats, yet they were leaders in the movement. The expansionist program of these people must be explained in other terms. When one comes to consider the imperialism of the present age, one is struck by the complete absence of the aristocratic heritage in Hitler and Mussolini. The case of Japan is somewhat different; there the aristocracy seems to .be directing the expansionist movement, but before it can be stated conclusively that Schumpeter's theory is applicable one would have to determine whether Japanese feudalism and European feudalism are comparable.

Even if Chamberlain had adopted a policy of imperialism as a result of his adoption of aristocratic tastes, it would be difficult to prove because one would be compelled to show that the reasons offered for the adoption of such a policy were mere rationalizations of a blind desire for expansion. Admitting that the reasons given were, in part, rationalizations, they may have been made necessary by the development of certain moral ideals which rendered a naked statement of policy—whatever it may have been—unwise.

Whatever may have been the moral ideals of the British people during the last half of the nineteenth century, there is reason to believe that they were lower at the time of Chamberlain's ascendancy than they were when Disraeli was in power. This probably accounts for the fact that Chamberlain had more success than Disraeli with his policy of imperialism. Perhaps that is why Chamberlain became the chief figure among the British statesmen who pursued a policy of imperialism. Perhaps that is why Chamberlain has been charged with being more vain and cruel than Disraeli in fostering the expansion and consolidation of the Empire. Perhaps that is why Chamberlain was able to act completely without scruples in his work; perhaps that accounts for the accusation that he "brutalized and vulgarized" the work of Disraeli,[26] whom he had accepted as his model. Chamberlain aso succeeded to the place held by "Dizzy" in the Queen's favor. Upon his return from America in 1888 Chamberlain received an autographed picture of Queen Victoria, the first such presentation that had occurred since a similar honor had been bestowed upon Disraeli.[27]

Although Lord Farrer, the chief civil servant in the Board of Trade during Chamberlain's presidency, stated that he never considered his chief an orthodox free trader and, although Dilke has recorded that he found his friend to have great faith in the principles of reciprocity, Chamberlain was considered to be a free trader until the latter phases of his career. The change in Chamberlain's attitude on free trade was a gradual one. He was perhaps influenced to some extent by political reasons. After 1885 he found that in his home city of Birmingham it became increasingly difficult to carry the elections due to the opposition of the Fair Traders. The commercial and industrial interests of

Birmingham were also losing faith in free trade arguments and were demanding alterations in Britain's trade policy. While Chamberlain did not at first advocate changing the trade policies of Great Britain, he did, as was seen in Chapter IV, urge a tightening of the bonds of Empire to encourage, among other things, intra-Imperial trade. This was in 1889. It was not, however, until he found that the Dominions would co-operate only on a basis of a protective tariff for Great Britain that he deserted free trade and became a Protectionist. After he had argued that the greater unity of the Empire would increase trade, it was but natural that he should expand the statement and say that, since trade follows the flag, new colonies were necessary to provide the needed raw materials and the adequate markets for British manufacturers, and that the Government existed to procure commerce for the industries of the country.

All these arguments have been used to show that imperialism is chiefly an economic phenomenon. The first well-known work tending to prove this thesis was Hobson's *Imperialism;* Professor W. L. Langer is of the opinion, however, that Hobson gleaned his argument from an article by an American economist, Charles A. Conant.[28] Conant's contention was that capitalism had reached that stage in its development in which more goods existed than the market demanded, and in which more savings existed than the investment world could absorb. In order to relieve this excess, the great industrial countries had to exploit those areas which had not "felt the pulse of modern progress."[29]

Hobson discussed the psychological, religious, moral, and other factors which contributed to imperialism, but he believed that the economic factor was the determinant cause of that policy. He declared that the apparent spontaneity of imperialism was an illusion—in reality it was controlled and guided by financiers. He stated that although Chamberlain considered himself a free agent working for the aggrandizement of the Empire, he was really the unwitting instrument of the "generals of finance."[30]

The Marxists have written more concerning the economic basis of imperialism than any other school of writers, but they do not agree among themselves on the interpretation of imperialism other than to declare that imperialism springs from capitalism. Marx himself did not state a theory of imperialism. He discussed the old colonialism which belonged to the pre-capitalistic accumulation of wealth. The only time he used the word "Imperialismus" was in speaking of the Empire of Napoleon III. Writing in the *Paris Commune,* he said:

"Imperialism is . . . the most prostitute and ultimate form of the state power which nascent middle class society has commenced to elaborate as a means of its own emancipation from feudalism, and full-grown bourgeois society has already finally transformed it into a means for the enslavement of labor by capital."[31]

In discussing imperialism the Marxists have not been able to prove their contentions by reference to the writings of Karl Marx; they have never agreed that imperialism is a stage of capitalism or merely a policy thereof.

Karl Kautsky, one of the leading German Marxists, declared imperialism was the product of a highly developed stage of capitalism in which the capitalistic nations annexed more and more territory in order to dispose of surplus goods. Rosa Luxemburg, another German Marxist, believed that the expansion of capitalism in non-capitalistic lands prolonged the existence of the capitalistic structure. Hilferding said capitalism sought exclusive control over the domestic market by building tariff barriers; it sought to expand the area of its exclusive control through the acquisition which it included within its tariff barriers. For Lenin, imperialism was the monopolistic stage of capitalism, the stage in which the great financial interests controlled capitalism. It was in this period—the dying stage of capitalism—that the export of capital and the acquisition of colonial markets was most essential. In this stage the leading capitalistic countries divided the territory of the earth among themselves.[32] He stated that the non-economic causes for imperialism might be important, but he did not discuss them since they were subordinate to the economic cause.[33]

Whether or not the facts in the case fit the Marxian argument is a matter of some conjecture. According to Lenin, "the export of capital was one of the essential economic bases of imperialism."[34] The purpose of acquiring colonies was to offer an outlet for the export of surplus capital. In the year in which the current period of imperialism began—1872—the export of capital from Great Britain had reached a new high of 83.5 millions of pounds sterling; however, the export of capital then began to decline. There was even an import of capital in 1876, 1877, and 1878. For the next decade a gradual rise in capital export became apparent, the peak of 1872 being almost reached in 1890. This rise was followed by a decline during the next decade, but in 1902 another period of increased export began, the increase being due to demands from other European countries and the United States rather than from the newly acquired colonies.[35] This seems to indicate that during the last three decades of the nineteenth century and in the opening years of the present one there was no pressing need for new areas in which to invest capital. Opportunity for investment in domestic enterprises and in the more highly industrialized nations seemed sufficient to absorb the available capital.

Turning from the figures on capital export to the general trade figures, one finds that in general when British trade with foreign countries increased, its trade with the colonies[36] also increased; when the trade with foreign countries decreased the trade with the colonies did likewise. The British imports from the colonies from 1880 to 1889 do not fit this picture exactly, for in the first five years of this decade the imports from foreign countries increased, while the imports from the colonies decreased. In the second five years the imports from foreign countries decreased but the imports from the colonies remained steady.[37] If trade with foreign countries followed the general trend in world trade, one might then assume that the trade of Great Britain with her colonies rose and fell as did world trade in general.

In general, the trade with the Dominions increased steadily through the last three decades of the nineteenth century regardless of the rise or decline of British trade with foreign countries. However, from 1885 to 1889, imports from the Dominions declined along with the imports from the foreign countries. From 1890 to 1894 exports of the United Kingdom to the Dominions declined although the exports to foreign countries increased within this period. The imports from India tended to decline during this period; the exports to India tended to increase.[38]

Since the trade with the colonies increased or decreased along with increases and decreases in the foreign trade it might be possible to reason that the increase in the colonial trade in the last decade of the century was the result of a general increase in trade rather than the result of a program of expansion. Be that as it may, it is not wise to maintain that a desire for increased trade did not contribute to the program of expansion. Although British trade tended to increase in the last decades of the nineteenth century, if one compares the trade per capita in 1870 with the trade per capita in 1900, one sees that the trade per capita had declined.[39] Although world trade was increasing during this period, the percentage of that trade which fell to Great Britain was declining. The greater part of the total world trade seemed to be in the hands of the rising industrial states, particularly the United States and Germany. No doubt there was a feeling on the part of British industry that its position of leadership was being threatened. This being so, the commercial class may have felt that additional colonies were necessary to provide the markets which seemed to be in jeopardy.

British trade with the colonies did increase during the period of territorial expansion. Moreover the trade with the colonies increased at a greater rate than British trade with foreign countries, which would indicate that some other factor than a general increase in trade was responsible for that higher rate of increase. It is natural to assume, therefore, that Chamberlain and his associates were correct when they argued that trade followed the flag. However, one ought to remember that whenever Great Britian acquired a colony it lost a portion of its foreign trade. That is to say, before Ashantee became a part of the Empire the trade with that area was listed as foreign trade, afterwards it was listed as colonial trade. The well-nigh unanswerable question arises from that fact: would the trade of Great Britian with Ashantee and the other newly acquired colonies have increased in the same degree had those colonies remained foreign countries?

This question is further complicated by the tariff factor. Since Great Britain's rivals extended their Protective systems to their colonial possessions each addition to those possessions meant an additional tariff barrier to British trade. From this followed the natural impulse of the British Government to acquire colonies in order to prevent this. Chamberlain's argument, at first, was that such acquisitions increased the free trade area of the world. This argument lost its force when he adopted Protection. However great or small the increase in the colonial trade during the last three decades of the nineteenth century and however small the proportion of colonial trade as compared to the total trade, it is very probable that the commercial interests believed the total trade would have been smaller had not Great Britian acquired the colonies it did.

One of the reasons for the increase in the trade of Great Britian was the increasing need for iron and steel goods and the coal necessary to process these products. This resulted in a total net gain for British trade. It is interesting to note in this respect that the increase in exports of iron and steel and coal was due to demands from the more highly industrialized nations, particularly Germany and the United States, the trade rivals of Great Britian. While Germany and the United States increased their purchases of these goods from Great Britain, those very purchases made them less and less dependent on Great Britian for their textiles. During these years Britain was searching for new textile markets, which the commercial interests hoped to find in the newly acquired colonies. Although Great Britian might expect to increase its iron, steel, and coal trade in developing the possessions, the heavy industries were not suffering the same slump as the textile industry.

The plea that the extension of the Empire would prove an economic advantage was only one of several reasons which caused Chamberlain to adopt a policy of imperialism.[40] Another reason not previously mentioned was personal ambition. It is difficult to weigh the importance which hope for political advancement played in the formation of Chamberlain's policy. However, one cannot read the documents of his associates without being impressed with the fact that they considered him to be driven by such a desire. Gladstone told Bryce that Chamberlain was " a most dangerous man, restless, ambitious, unscrupulous."[41] John Mackinon Robertson has left this characterization:

> "Chamberlain could not live out of the world of affairs, could not face isolation, could not make for himself a refuge of thought or contemplation. He had, in fact, no philosophy of life; he had only instincts, appetites, ambitions, prejudices, hatreds, energies, the stock-in-trade of an average public man, in a much fuller than average measure;and public life, action, power, were to him as the breath of life in his nostrils. After his years of pride of place [prior to the Home-Rule fight], the prospect of exclusion from office for many years seems to have progressively maddened him. His little appetite for study had been easily glutted, and his conservatory was his one private occupation; he must be a politician or nothing."[42]

Even some of those who deny that Chamberlain was moved primarily by ambition and lust for power admit that this drive was present. Their chief argument advanced to indicate that it was not a primary motive in his career was that he resigned from the Cabinet in 1886.[43] The contention is that in resigning he sacrificed his ambitions for his convictions.

The bitterness of the struggle over Home Rule caused Chamberlain to lose interest in domestic affairs. If he was to continue in politics he had to choose some other field of endeavor. In adopting a policy of expansion and consolidation of the Empire he may have been motivated by a belief that the adoption of such a policy offered more opportunity for political advancement than the adoption of any other policy. Admitting that Chamberlain was moved by personal ambition, it is difficult to determine whether this ambition was a major or a minor factor in the development of his imperialism. It is difficult, if not impossible, to determine whether the reasons Chamberlain advanced for his policy were used as rationalizations of his personal desires, or whether he was really sincere in advancing his argument for expansion, unconscious of any ambition for personal advancement. Personal ambition is a factor which influences the careers of many public men. It was present in the career of Disraeli when he launched the policy of imperialism carried on by Chamberlain. It was a moving factor in the career of another Imperialist of the times, Cecil Rhodes. That it also motivated Joseph Chamberlain is not surprising.

The factors that influenced Chamberlain in his policy of imperialism were, in a large measure, the same factors that influenced the thinking of all people in the latter years of the century. It has already been seen how the writings of Darwin influenced the thought of the day. The rise of social Darwinism coupled with the spread of the false racial doctrines first promulgated by De Gobineau and further elaborated by Houston Stewart Chamberlain colored the whole intellectual background. It resulted in the glorification of force and the brutalization of the finer human qualities. During the eighteenth century philosophers had evolved a systematic statement of the dawn of a new era. These thinkers may have been visionary, they may have exaggerated the rationality of man, but as a result of their efforts, people began to hope for the gradual betterment of man and his environment.

The Thermidor of the French Revolution and the destruction caused by the Napoleonic Wars may have cast some doubt on the validity of the argument of the eighteenth-century thinkers, but that their influence was still potent was evidenced by the Revolutions of 1848, the triumph of free trade in Great Britian, and the mid-century strength of Liberalism. By 1870, however, the influence of Liberalism seemed to be declining; an era of *Realpolitik* was being ushered in along with an era of crude and blatant industrialism. Into such a culture the entrance of theories which gave a "scientific" justification for brutality and thinly disguised theft was more than welcome.

The environment was ideal for Gladstone's *homme autoritaire,* i. e., Chamberlain. A product of industrial Birmingham, he was devoted to its materialistic desires. He readily absorbed the racial doctrines of his friend, Charles Dilke. An intensely patriotic Englishman, he desired to make Britian's superiority conceded by all. He accepted the prevailing thought of his day and used it to further his desire for the wider extension of British political and economic control in the world. If he stressed the superiority of the British race and its civilizing mission, he was but giving voice to the prevailing opinion in England. The language he spoke was understood and accepted not only by the associates of Professors Kidd and Pearson but also by the vast audience which fed on the work of that poetic apostle of imperialism, Rudyard Kipling.

The culture of the late nineteenth century was a cauldron in which an evil brew simmered. It boiled over into World War I. It seems reasonable to believe that that should have sobered man and made him do something about the evils in a culture which gives rise to such twin devils as nationalism and imperialism, but apparently that was not the case.

REFERENCES

[1]Dilke, *op. cit.*, v, vi.
[2]*Ibid.*, II, 382, 310, 404.
[3]*Ibid.*, 395.
[4]*Ibid.*, 407.
[5]Charles Dilke, *Problems of Greater Britain* (London & New York, 1890), 695-6.
[6]*Ibid.*, 697.
[7]*Ibid.*, 629.
[8]Walter Bagehot, *Physics and Politics* (New York, 1908), 43.
[9]See Sontag, *op. cit.*, 100 ff. for a discussion of Bagehot and his influence on English life.
[10]*Cf.* Hobson, *op. cit.*, 136.
[11]Benjamin Kidd, *Social Evolution* (New York & London, 1894), 34.
[12]See *ibid.*, 310-29 for Kidd's own summary of his ideas. His *Control of the Tropics* (New York, 1898) added little, if anything, to his argument.
[13]Chamberlain used Kidd's writings to support his argument for colonial expansion. See J. Chamberlain, "Recent Developments of Policy in the United States," *Scribners*, v. 24, p. 678.
[14]*Edwardian England* (London, 1933), 245.
[15]John Seeley, *Expansion of England* (London, 1883), 10-89.
[16]Berard, *op. cit.*, 44.
[17]G. M. Benedict, *English Imperialism in the Last Decade of the Nineteenth Century* (Unpublished doctoral thesis, Harvard University, 1933), 283-4.
[18]V. L. Parrington, *Main Currents in American Thought* (New York, 1930), III, 167. Not all of the poetry of the day was in support of imperialism. Oscar Wilde in his "Ave Imperatrix" had cried out against it. Wilde's poetry was not well-received, however, until after the turn of the century.
[19]Julius W. Pratt, *The Expansionists of 1898* (Baltimore, 1936). Chapter I contains a summary of the views of Fiske, Strong, Burgess, and others.
[20]Hobson, *op. cit.*, 136-74.
[21]L. T. Hobhouse, *Democracy and Reaction* (New York, 1905).
[22]Robertson, *op. cit.*, 51.
[23]Austen Chamberlain, *Politics from Inside* (London, 1936), 509.
[24]Russell, *loc. cit.*, 314.
[25]Joseph Schumpeter, "Zur Soziologie der Imperialismus," *Archiv fur Socialwissenschaft und Socialpolitik*, v. 46, no. 1, 1918-1919.
[26]Ouida, "Joseph Chamberlain," *Living Age*, 1900, ser. 7, v. 7, p. 405.
[27]E. H. S. Escott, "The Evolution of Joseph Chamberlain," *British Review*, 1914, v. 7, p. 339.
[28]Langer, *loc. cit.*, 102.
[29]Charles A. Conant, "The Economic Basis of Imperialism," *North American Review*, 1898, v. 167, p. 236-40.
[30]J. A. Hobson, *Capitalism and Imperialism in South Africa* (New York, 1900), 29-30.

[31]Quoted in E. M. Winslow, "Marxian, Liberal and Sociological Theories of Imperialism," *Journal of Political Economy*, 1931, XXXIX, 717.

[32]V. L. Lenin, *Imperialism* (New York, 1929), 52-82.

[33]*Ibid.*, 3.

[34]*Ibid.*, 83; *cf.* also 47.

[35]C. K. Hobson, *The Export of Capital* (New York, 1914), 204 ff.

[36]In these paragraphs devoted to the analysis of British trade, "colonies" refer to all British possessions exclusive of India and the Dominions.

[37]See data regarding exports and imports in *The Statistical Abstract of the United Kingdom* (London, 1897-1903).

[38]*Ibid.*

[39]J. A. Hobson, *Imperialism, A Study* (London, 1938), 31.

[40]See *infra*, Chapter V, for a discussion of the influence of the racial factor on Chamberlain's policies.

[41]H. A. L. Fisher, *James Bryce* (London, 1927), I, 216.

[42]Robertson, *op. cit.*, 39.

[43]E. T. Cook, "Mr. Chamberlain," *Contemporary Review*, 1914, v. 106, p. 159.

Bibliography

I. *Government Documents*

Accounts and Papers, LVII, C. 7917, 1896. Further Correspondence Relating to Affairs in Ashanti.

Accounts and Papers, LVII, C. 7918, 1896. Further Correspondence Relating to Affairs in Ashanti.

Accounts and Papers, LIX, C. 7932, 1896. Correspondence Relative to the Transfer of British Bechuanaland to Cape Colony.

Accounts and Papers, LIX, C. 7933, 1896. Correspondence on the Subject of Recent Disturbances in the South African Republic.

Accounts and Papers, LIX, C. 8063, 1896. Correspondence Relating to the Recent Disturbances in the South African Republic.

Accounts and Papers, LX, C. 8449, 1897. Despatch from Mr. Chamberlain to the Governors of the Colonies and the High Commissioner of Cyprus on the Trade of the British Empire and Foreign Competition; and the Replies Thereto.

Accounts and Papers, LV, C. 8797, 1898. Correspondence Relating to Native Disturbances in Bechuanaland.

Accounts and Papers, LIX, C. 8922, 1898. Commission and Instruction to Sir David P. Chalmers as Her Majesty's Commissioner to Enquire into the Native Insurrection.

Accounts and Papers, LX, C. 9388, 1899. Report by Her Majesty's Commissioners and Correspondence on the Subject of the Sierre Leon Protectorate.

Accounts and Papers, LXVII, C. 1299, 1902. Papers Relative to a Conference Between the Secretary of State for the Colonies and the Prime Ministers of the Self-Governing Colonies, June to August, 1902.

Hansard's Parliamentary Debates, Third Series, v. 227–356; Fourth Series, v. 1–151, 1876–1905.

II. *Newspapers*

The Times (London), 1884–1905.

III. *General Works*

A. *Books*

Allin, Cephas Daniel, *Colonial Participation in Imperial Warfare—Australasia*, Kingston, 1926.

Bagehot, Walter, *Physics and Politics*, New York, 1908.

Benedict, Gordon Marsh, *English Imperialism in the Last Decade of the Nineteenth Century*, unpublished doctoral thesis, Harvard University, 1933.

Bérard, Victor, *British Imperialism and Commercial Policy*, London, New York and Bombay, 1906.

Binkley, Robert C., *Realism and Nationalism, 1852–1871*, New York and London, 1935.

Bodelsen, C. A. G., *Studies in Mid-Victorian Imperialism*, London, 1924.

Bukharin, N., *Imperialism and World Economy*, New York, 1929.

Cecil, Lady Gwendolen, *Life of Robert Marquis of Salisbury*, 4 v., London, 1921–1932.

Crewe, The Marquess of, *Lord Rosebery*, 2 v., London, 1931.

Currey, Charles Herbert, *British Colonial Policy, 1783–1915*, Oxford, 1926.

Curzon, George, *Problems of the Far East*, London, 1894.

Dilke, Sir C. W., *Greater Britain*, New York, 1869.

Dilke, Sir C. W., *Problems of Greater Britain*, London and New York, 1890.

Dugdale, Blanche E. C., *Arthur James Balfour*, 2 v., London, 1936.

Edwards, J. Hugh, *David Lloyd George, The Man and the Statesman*, 2 v., New York, 1929.

Ensor, R. C. K., *England, 1870–1914*, Oxford, 1936.

Fisher, H. A. L., *James Bryce*, 2 v., London, 1927.

Fitzmaurice, Edmond George Petty-Fitzmaurice, *The Life of Granville George Leverson Gower, Lord Granville*, 2 v., New York and London, 1905.

Gardiner, Alfred George, *Life of Sir William Harcourt*, 2 v., London, 1923.

Gastrell, William Shaw, *Our Trade in the World in Relation to Foreign Competition, 1885–1895*, London, 1897.

Goldman, Charles Sidney (ed.), *The Empire and the Century*, London, 1905.

Gould, Francis Carruthers, *Political Caricatures 1903*, London, 1903.

Gwynn, Stephen and Tuckwell, G. M., *The Life of the Right Hon. Sir Charles W. Dilke*, 2 v., New York, 1917.

Hammond, L. J., *Gladstone and the Irish Nation*, London, 1938.

Headlam, Cecil, *The Milner Papers*, 2 v., London, 1931–1933.

Hobhouse, Leonard T., *Democracy and Reaction*, New York, 1905.

Hobson, J. A., *Capitalism and Imperialism in South Africa*, New York, 1900.

Hobson, J. A., *Imperialism, A Study*, London, 1905.

Hobson, J. A., *The Psychology of Jingoism*, London, 1901.

Hoffman, Ross J. S., *Great Britain and the German Trade Rivalry, 1875–1914*, Philadelphia, 1933.

Holland, Bernard, *The Life of Spencer Compton, Eighth Duke of Devonshire*, 2 v., London, 1911.

Kidd, Benjamin, *Control of the Tropics*, New York, 1898.

Kidd, Benjamin, *Social Evolution*, London, 1895.

Knaplund, Paul, *Gladstone and British Imperial Policy*, London, 1927.

Knaplund, Paul, *Gladstone's Foreign Policy*, New York and London, 1935.

Kohn, Hans, *Force or Reason*, Cambridge, Mass., 1936.

Langer, W. L., *The Diplomacy of Imperialism*, 2 v., New York, 1935.

Laski, Harold J., *Democracy in Crisis*, Chapel Hill, N. C., 1933.

Lawson, Sir Wilfred and Gould, F. C., *Cartoons in Rhyme and Line*, London, 1905.

Lenin, N., *Imperialism*, Detroit, 1924.

Lovell, Reginald Ivan, *The Struggle for South Africa*, New York, 1934.

Lynch, Arthur, *Human Documents; Character Sketches of Representative Men and Women of the Time*, London, 1896.

Mill, John Stuart, *England and Ireland*, London, 1868.

Milner, A., *England in Egypt*, London, 1892.

Monypenny, William Flavelle and Buckle, George Earle, *The Life of Benjamin Disraeli*, 6 v., New York, 1910–1920.

Morley, John, *Life of W. E. Gladstone*, 3 v., London, 1903.

Morley, John, Viscount, *Recollections*, 2 v., New York, 1917.

Pratt, Julius W., *Expansionists of 1898*, Baltimore, 1936.

Schulze-Gavernitz, G. von, *Britischer Imperialismus und Englisher Freihandel*, Leipzig, 1906.

Seeley, John R., *Expansion of England*, London, 1883.

Sontag, Raymond J., *Germany and England*, New York, 1938.

Spender, J. A. and Asquith, Cyril, *Life of Herbert Henry Asquith, Lord of Oxford and Asquith*, 2 v., London, 1932.

Staley, Eugene, *War and the Private Investor*, Garden City, N. Y., 1935.

Walker, Eric A., *A History of South Africa*, London, 1928.

Woolf, Leonard, *Economic Imperialism*, London, 1921.

Woolf, Leonard, *Imperialism and Civilization*, New York, 1928.

B. *Articles*

Conant, Charles A., "The Economic Basis of Imperialism," *North American Review*, 1898, vol. 167, pp. 326–40.

Hobson, J. A., "Scientific Basis of Imperialism," *Political Science Quarterly*, 1902, vol. XVII, pp. 460–89.

Hovde, B. J., "Socialistic Theories of Imperialism Prior to the Great War," *Journal of Political Economy*, 1928, vol. XXXVI, pp. 569–91.

Langer, William L., "A Critique of Imperialism," *Foreign Affairs*, 1935, vol. XIV, pp. 102–119.

Wagner, Donald O., "British Economists and the Empire," *Political Science Quarterly*, 1932, vol. XLVII, pp. 57–74.

Winslow, E. M., "Marxian, Liberal and Sociological Theories of Imperialism," *Journal of Political Economy*, 1931, vol. XXXIX, pp. 713–58.

IV. *Chamberlainiana*

A. *Books and Pamphlets*

Anthony, Charles, *Mr. Chamberlain's Proposals*, London, 1903.

Asquith, Herbert Henry, *Trade and Empire*, London, 1903.

Bijoux, J. O., *Chamberlain: étude*, Port-Louis, West Indies, 1904.

Boyd, Charles W. (ed.), *Mr. Chamberlain's Speeches*, 2 v., London, 1914.

Braude, Bernhard, *Die Grundlagen und die Grenzen der Chamberlainismus.*

Studien zur Tarifreformbewegung in Gegenwartigen England, Zurich, 1904.

Chamberlain, Austen, *Down the Years*, London, 1935.

Chamberlain, Austen, *Politics from Inside*, London, 1936.

Chamberlain, Joseph, *Foreign and Colonial Speeches*, London, 1897.

Chamberlain, Joseph, *Home Rule and the Irish Question*, London, 1887.

Chamberlain, Joseph, *Imperial Union and Tariff Reform*, London, 1903.

Chamberlain, Joseph, *Imperialism and Preferential Trade*, Birmingham, 1904.

Chamberlain, Joseph, *Mr. Chamberlain's Defense of the British Troops in South Africa Against Foreign Slander*, London, 1902.

Chamberlain, Joseph, *The Policy of Imperial Preference*, Birmingham, 1903.

Chamberlain, Joseph, *Speeches on the Irish Question*, London, 1890.

Chamberlain, Joseph, *Tariff Reform and the Agricultural Industry*, Birmingham, 1904.

Chamberlain, Joseph, *Tariff Reform and the Colonial Conference*, Birmingham, 1904.

Chamberlain, Joseph, *The Radical Platform, Speeches, 1885*, Edinburgh and London, 1885.

[Chamberlain]

Anglo-Saxon (pseud.), *Joseph, the Deliverer of the Land of Egypt*, London, 1903.

The Chamberlain Birthday Book, London, 1898.

Chamberlain, Der Lügner. Deutsche Volksproteste gegen die Verläumdungen des Englischer Colonialminister Chamberlain, Leipzig, 1901.

A Chamberlain Picture Book. Being No. 1 of a Special General Election Issue of "Picture-Politics," London, 1895.

Correspondence Between W. G. M. Betton of Jamaica and the Rt. Hon. J. Chamberlain. Coolie Immigration into Jamaica, Liverpool, 1902 (?).

Mr. Daniel Creedy, M.P. An Extravaganza Intended to Satirize Mr. Chamberlain, London, 1884.

Defeat and Retreat . . . Letters From Joseph, London, 1883.

Der Mörder der Kinder und Frauen, Munich, 1901.

The Fiscal Piper of Brun, London, 1904.

Not for Joe—A Political Medley, London, 1888.

Past and Present, Glasgow, 1887.

Playing Mr. Chamberlain's Game, London, 1903.

The Radical Programme, London, 1885.

The Return to Sanity, London, 1903.

Talus, *Now or Never!* A Letter (on the political crisis) to the Rt. Hon. . . . (i.e., J. Chamberlain), London, 1886.

Creswicke, Louis, *The Life of the Right Hon. J. Chamberlain*, 4 v., London, 1904–1905.

Crosland, T. W. H., *A Looking Glass for Mr. Chamberlain*, London, 1903.

Cunningham, William, *The Case Against Free Trade*, London, 1901.

Denison, George Anthony, *Mr. Chamberlain*, London, 1886.

Draper, J., *The Statesman and the Bishop*, London, 1904.

Drumcavil, David o', *Farthing Joe*, Glasgow, 1904.

Enzberg, E. von, *Protest gegen Chamberlain*, Berlin, 1901.

Farrer, Thomas Henry, *The Neo-Protection Scheme of the Rt. Hon. J. Chamberlain*, London, 1896.

Filon, Augustin, *Profils Anglais: Randolph Churchill, J. Chamberlain*, Paris, 1893.

Fletcher, J. S., *Owd Poskitt, His Opinion on Mr. Chamberlain . . . and . . . English Trade*, London, 1903.

Fowell, Frank, *Potted Policies, J. Chamberlain*, London, 1912.

Furniss, Harry, *"Our Joe,"* London, 1903.

Garvin, James Louis, *The Life of J. Chamberlain*, 3 v., New York and London, 1932.

Gazeau, Jacques, *L'Imperialisme Anglais. Son Evolution; Carlyle, Seeley, Chamberlain*, Paris, 1903.

Griffith, George, *With Chamberlain Through South Africa*, London, 1903.

Gulley, Elsie Elizabeth, *J. Chamberlain and Social Reform*, New York, 1928.

Hammond, W. J., *Thoughts on Mr. Chamberlain's Proposed Policy*, London, 1903.

Harrison, Henry, *Parnell, Joseph Chamberlain and Mr. Garvin*, London, 1938.

Herring, Paul, *The Wrong Mr. Chamberlain. The Misadventure of Mr. Timothy Gedge. A Fiscal Farce*, Bristol, 1904.

Housman, Laurence, *Dethronements; Imaginary Portraits of Political Characters*, London, 1922.

Iles, J. H. and Sheff, L., *Souvenir of Mr. Chamberlain's South African Tour*, Wolverhampton, 1903.

Jeyes, Samuel Henry, *Mr. Chamberlain, His Life and Public Career*, London, 1903.

Jeyes, Samuel Henry, *The Right Hon. J. Chamberlain*, London, 1896.

Jonas, Erich, *Chamberlains Handelspolitik Projecjte, ihre Grundlagen und ihre Grenzen*, Sagen, 1906.

Junior, D., *Joe Chamberlain, Vroolyke Vordracht op Bruilsoften en andere Partijen*, Gron, 1902.

Leech, H. J., *The Rt. Hon. J. Chamberlain*, Manchester, 1885.

Lucy, Henry W. (ed.), *Speeches of the Right Hon. J. Chamberlain*, London and New York, 1885.

Macgoun, Arch., *The Revenue Tariff with the Empire. Canadian Chapters on Mr. Chamberlain's Fiscal Policy*, Montreal, 1904.

Mackintosh, Alexander, *J. Chamberlain, An Honest Biography*, London, 1906.

Mackintosh, Alexander, *J. Chamberlain. On Both Sides. A Book of Contrasts*, London, 1905.

140 *Bibliography*

Mackintosh, Alexander, *The Story of Mr. Chamberlain's Life*, London, 1914.
Marriott, W. T., *The Liberal Party and Mr. Chamberlain*, London, 1884 (?).
Marris, N. Murrell, *The Right Hon. J. Chamberlain, The Man and the Statesman*, London, 1900.
Marris, N. Murrell, *Joseph Chamberlain, Imperialist, 1836–1906*, London, 1906.
Mathison, E., *The Principles of Foreign Exchange as Affecting Preferential Trade with the Colonies as Proposed by the Rt. Hon. J. Chamberlain*, Leeds and London, 1903.
Maycock, Sir William, *With Mr. Chamberlain in the United States and Canada, 1887–1888*, Toronto, 1914.
Mee, Arthur, *J. Chamberlain, A Romance of Modern Politics*, London, 1901.
Methuen, Algernon Methuen Marshall, *England's Ruin Discussed in Sixteen Letters to the Rt. Hon. J. Chamberlain, M.P.*, London, 1905.
Milner, Viscount and Others, *Life of Joseph Chamberlain*, London, 1914.
Moore, R. L., *Commissions and Travels of H.M.S. Good Hope*, Cape Town, 1903.
Mostyn, T., *The Joseph Jingle Book*, London (no date).
Pedder, H. C., *The Rt. Hon. J. Chamberlain. A Study of His Character as a Statesman*, London, 1902.
Perris, George Herbert, *The Protectionist Peril; an Examination of Mr. Chamberlain's Proposal*, London, 1903.
Peters, K., *Mr. Chamberlain's Zollreform und Deutschland*, Hanover, 1904.
Petrie, Sir Charles, *The Chamberlain Tradition*, London, 1938.
Prosch, ——, *Englands Verbrechen an Transvaal und Mr. Chamberlains Verleumdung der Deutsche Kriegsführung*, Offenbach, 1902.
Quick, Jonathan (pseud.), *Gulliver Joe*, London, 1903.
Robertson, John Mackinon, *Chamberlain: A Study*, London, 1905.
Robertson, John Mackinon, *The Collapse of Tariff Reform*, London, 1911.
Rodgers, E. and Moyle, E. J., *The Rt. Hon. J. Chamberlain. The Man of the Moment*, London, 1903.
Schubart, Frau Waldtraut, *Die Wirtschaftliche Selbstgenügsamkeit J. Chamberlains; ein Historisches Entwicklungsversuch*, Berlin, 1911.
Schwab, Marie (Koeglmayr), *Chamberlains Handelspolitik*, Jena, 1905.
Skottowe, Britiffe Constable, *Life of J. Chamberlain*, Birmingham, 1885.
Smith, Bartholomew, *Chamberlain and Chamberlainism; His Fiscal Proposal and Colonial Policy*, London, 1903.
Smith, J. Rigby, *Mr. Chamberlain's Defence of Colonial Protection*, London, 1903.
Stead, William Thomas, *Blastus, The King's Chamberlain*, London, 1896.
Stead, William Thomas, *Chamberlain, Conspirator or Statesman*, London, 1900.
Stead, William Thomas, *The History of the Mystery*, London, 1897.
Sutherland, J. C., *The Chamberlain Proposals from the Canadian Point of View*, Montreal, 1904.

Sykes, William, *Before Joseph Came into Egypt*, London, 1898.

Tariff Makers, London and New York, 1909.

Upward, Allen, *On His Majesty's Service; The Story of Tariff Reform*, London, 1903.

Vince, Charles Anthony, *Mr. Chamberlain's Proposals: What They Mean and What We Shall Gain by Them*, London, 1903.

Vince, Charles Anthony, *Trade and Empire. Tariff Reform and Common Sense*, Birmingham, 1908.

Walker, J., *Socialism Versus the Chamberlain Red Herring*, 1904.

Wallace, Arthur, *The Rt. Hon. J. Chamberlain*, 1900.

Warnotte, Daniel, *La Question Douanière en Angleterre la Première Campagne de M. Joseph Chamberlain, mai 1903–avril 1904*, Brussels, 1904.

Wilson, Herbert Wrigley, *Mr. Chamberlain's New Policy; Fifty Years of Free Trade*, London, 1903.

Woolf, ——, *Facts and Explanations in a Nutshell. The Chamberlain Policy, or Fiscal Reform at a Glance*, London, 1903.

B. *Articles*

Acland, F. A., "Chamberlain: Man and Statesman," *Booklover's Magazine*, 1903, vol. III, p. 21.

"Age of the Ostrich; Period of Make Believe," *Westminster Review*, 1906, vol. 165, pp. 355–69.

Allin, Cephas Daniel, "Joseph Chamberlain the Radical," *Mid-West Quarterly*, 1915, vol. 2, pp. 95–121.

"Balfour and Chamberlain," *Nation*, Oct. 8, 1903, vol. 77, pp. 277–78.

Beaugeard, Tiburce, "Chamberlain jugé par ses Compatriotes et par lui-même," *Nouvelle Revue*, n. s., vol. 1, pp. 481–98.

Bell, F. H., "Political Career of Joseph Chamberlain," *Citizen*, 1897, vol. 3, p. 280.

Bellot, H. H. L., "Chamberlain the Demagogue," *Westminster Review*, 1904, vol. 161, pp. 123–28.

Berard, Victor, "Joseph Chamberlain," *Revue de Paris*, 1898, année 5, vol. 6, pp. 747–84.

Birchenough, H., "Chamberlain as an Empire Builder," *Nineteenth Century*, 1902, vol. 51, pp. 360–68.

Bradley, Isaac, "Joseph Chamberlain," *Central Literary Magazine*, 1914, vol. 21, pp. 300–311.

Brand, W. F., "Chamberlainea. England before, during, and after the War," *Westminster Review*, 1901, vol. 155, pp. 262–73.

Brandt, M. von, "Joseph Chamberlain," *Deutsche Rundschau*, 1900, Jahrg. 26, vol. 102, pp. 388–413.

Brooks, S., "Chamberlain Programme," *Harper's Weekly*, July 18, 1903, vol. 47, p. 1186.

Brooks, S., "Joseph Chamberlain—Our Joe," *Independent*, Feb. 9, 1914, vol. 77, pp. 194–96.

Brooks, S., "Public Life of Joseph Chamberlain," *Harper's Weekly*, April 4, 1906, vol. 50, pp. 1098–99.

Burley, L. L., "Past and Future," *Independent*, 1903, vol. 55, pp. 2316–21.

Calchas, "The Man of Emergency," *Fortnightly Review*, 1903, vol. 77, n. s., vol. 71, pp. 181–93.

Chamberlain, A., "Joseph Chamberlain's Quotations," *Littell's Living Age*, April 19, 1924, vol. 321, pp. 760–63.

Chamberlain, Joseph, "Recent Developments of Policy in the United States and Their Relation to the Anglo-American Alliance," *Scribner's Magazine*, 1898, vol. 24, pp. 647–82.

"Chamberlain and Canada," *Outlook*, 1903, vol. 75, p. 22.

"Chamberlain and the Zollverein," *Westminster Review*, 1903, vol. 160, p. 1.

"Chamberlain and Ulster," *Westminster Review*, 1887, vol. 128, p. 1065.

"Chamberlain as Foreign Minister," *Fortnightly Review*, 1898, vol. 70, p. 317.

"Chamberlain's Career," *Nation*, July 9, 1914, vol. 99, pp. 35–36.

"Chamberlain, The Country and the Government," *Edinburgh Review*, 1905, vol. 202, pp. 264–76.

"Chamberlain's Knowledge of the Zollverein," *Westminster Review*, 1903, vol. 160, pp. 1–7.

"Chamberlain's Return from Africa and His Popularity," *Blackwood's Edinburgh Magazine*, 1903, vol. 173, pp. 550–53.

"Chamberlain's Triumph," *Gunton's Magazine*, 1900, vol. 19, pp. 405–17.

"Chamberlain's Views and Motives," *Outlook*, Feb. 17, 1906, vol. 82, pp. 337–38.

Cohen, Alexandre, "Mr. Chamberlain et la Caricature Anglais," *La Contemporaine*, 1901, pp. 309–25.

Coleridge, J. B. S., "England's Colonial Secretary," *North American Review*, 1903, vol. 176, pp. 832–45.

Cook, E. T., "Mr. Chamberlain," *Contemporary Review*, 1914, vol. 106, pp. 153–64.

Corbet, W. J., "An Impossible Premier," *Westminster Review*, 1904, vol. 161, pp. 145–60.

Courtney, Leonard, "Mr. Chamberlain's Balloon," *Contemporary Review*, 1903, vol. 84, pp. 265–76.

Cox, H., "Tariff Proposals of Joseph Chamberlain," *North American Review*, 1903, vol. 177, p. 1.

Crawford, L., "Political Career of Chamberlain," *Canadian Magazine*, 1914, vol. 43, pp. 426–27.

Currie, G. W., "Joseph Chamberlain and Ottawa," *Spectator*, April 21, 1933, vol. 150, p. 570.

D., W. T. T., "Joseph Chamberlain. In Memorium," *Kew Bulletin of Miscellaneous Information*, 1914, pp. 233–36.

Dicey, A. V., "Constitutional Aspects of Chamberlain's Journey to the Colonies," *Nation*, 1902, vol. 75, p. 477.

"English Protectionist Leader," *Outlook*, Nov. 7, 1903, vol. 75, pp. 572–73.

Escott, E. H. S., "The Evolution of Joseph Chamberlain," *British Review*, 1914, vol. 7, pp. 321–41.

"Fall of Balfour's Government," *Edinburgh Review*, 1906, vol. 203, pp. 263–79.

Fox, G. A., "The Vagaries of Distinguished Politicians," *Home Rule Union Leaflet*, no. 27.

"A French View of Chamberlain," *Saturday Review*, 1889, vol. 68, p. 584.

Garvin, J. L., "Mr. Chamberlain," *National Review*, 1907, vol. 49, pp. 845–96.

Garvin, J. L., "Secret of Mr. Chamberlain's Power," *Littell's Living Age*, Sept. 14, 1907, vol. 254, pp. 643–51.

Godkin, E. L., "Colonial Schemes," *Nation*, 1895, vol. 61, p. 443.

Gorst, J. E., "Tariff Proposals of Joseph Chamberlain," *North American Review*, 1903, vol. 177, p. 161.

Goschen, Viscount, "Tariff Proposals of Joseph Chamberlain," *Eclectic Magazine*, 1903, vol. 141, p. 434.

"Great Consult," *Edinburgh Review*, 1905, vol. 201, pp. 255–70.

"The Greatest Colonial Minister," *Fortnightly Review*, 1902, vol. 78, p. 913.

Guyot, Y., "Chamberlain in the Light of French Experience," *Fortnightly Review*, 1903, vol. 80, p. 1.

Guyot, Y. and Others, "The Tariff Proposals of Joseph Chamberlain," *Fortnightly Review*, 1903, vol. 80, p. 193.

Harris, G. B., "Chamberlain and Birmingham—The Political Riddle," *Fortnightly Review*, 1906, vol. 86, pp. 18–32.

Hobman, J. B., "Political Sir Willoughby Patterne," *Westminster Review*, 1901, vol. 156, pp. 133–37.

Hopkins, J. C., "Joseph Chamberlain," *Canadian Magazine*, 1895, vol. 6, p. 169.

Hopkins, T. M., "Chamberlain as a Tory Minister," *Westminster Review*, 1899, vol. 152, p. 117.

Hunt, L., "Chamberlain and Canada," *Canadian Magazine*, 1903, vol. 22, pp. 130–37.

"Intellectual Supremacy," *Canadian Magazine*, 1906, vol. 26, pp. 290–91.

"Joseph Chamberlain and Eugène Clemençeau," *Saturday Review*, 1894, vol. 79, p. 373.

"Joseph Chamberlain and the Irish Bill," *Saturday Review*, 1886, vol. 61, p. 562.

"Joseph Chamberlain on Trade," *Spectator*, 1894, vol. 74, p. 453.

Keane, Hilda, "Mr. Siddon and Mr. Chamberlain," *Empire Review*, 1903, vol. 6, pp. 9–12.

Longley, J. W., "Canada and the Chamberlain Movement," *Canadian Magazine*, 1904, vol. 22, pp. 232–36.

Lyon, J. M., "Chamberlain," *Westminster Review*, 1903, vol. 161, p. 97.

Lucy, H. W., "Joseph Chamberlain," *Independent*, 1900, vol. 52, p. 829.

Lucy, H. W., "Joseph Chamberlain; a Contemporary's Estimate," *Nation*, July 30, 1914, vol. 99, pp. 127–28.

Lucy, H. W., "Sixty Years in the Wilderness," *Littell's Living Age*, Jan. 16, 1909, vol. 260, pp. 152–56.

McInnis, E., "The Imperial Problem in the Minds of Chamberlain and His Successors," *Canadian Historical Review*, 1935, vol. 16, pp. 65–70.

Malcolm, I., "Chamberlain; the Second Phase," *Quarterly Review*, 1933, vol. 260, pp. 261–74.

"Master Worker," *Review of Reviews*, 1903, vol. 28, pp. 722–23.

Mather, F. J., Jr., "Showing Him Out," *Nation*, 1904, vol. 80, p. 240.

Maxse, F. A., "In Defense of Chamberlain," *National Review*, 1893, vol. 22, p. 104.

Maynaham, F. E., "Chamberlain's Visit to America," *National Magazine*, 1899, vol. 11, p. 593.

Middlemore, T., "Joseph Chamberlain Deductively Considered," *Economic Review*, 1905, vol. 15, p. 28.

"Mistakes of Joseph Chamberlain," *Fortnightly Review*, 1899, vol. 72, p. 705.

Mitchell, T. W., "The Development of Mr. Chamberlain's Fiscal Policy," *Annals of the American Academy of Political and Social Science*, 1904, publication no. 405.

Moireau, Auguste, "Le Triumph de Chamberlain," *Revue Politique et Littéraire*, 1900, ser. 4, vol. 14, pp. 556–60.

Morgan, Ben H., "Joseph Chamberlain; the Man and His Ideals," *Britannic Review*, 1914, pp. 439–49.

"Mr. Chamberlain," *Spectator*, July 11, 1914, vol. 113, pp. 45–46.

"Mr. Chamberlain's Fiscal Policy," *Quarterly Review*, 1903, vol. 198, pp. 246–78.

"Mr. Chamberlain's Land Policy," *Spectator*, Oct. 23, 1909, vol. 103, p. 634.

Nelson, H. L., "Tariff Proposals of Joseph Chamberlain," *North American Review*, 1903, vol. 177, p. 183.

Nelson, K. G., "Chamberlain at Home," *Harper's Bazaar*, May 12, 1900, vol. 33, pp. 88–90.

Notestein, W., "Joseph Chamberlain and the Tariff Reform," *Sewanee Review*, 1917, vol. 25, pp. 40–56.

Ogden, R., "Antidote for Chamberlain," *Nation*, 1902, vol. 76, p. 450.

Ogden, R., "Chamberlain and Kruger," *Nation*, 1901, vol. 73, p. 146.

Ogden, R., "Chamberlain and the Premiers," *Nation*, 1902, vol. 75, p. 26.

Ogden, R., "Chamberlain in South Africa," *Nation*, 1902, vol. 76, p. 106.

Ogden, R., "Tariff Proposals of Joseph Chamberlain," *Nation*, 1903, vol. 77, p. 296.

Ouida, "Joseph Chamberlain," *Littell's Living Age*, 1900, ser. 7, vol. 7, pp. 401–407.

Ouida, "Joseph Chamberlain," *Nuova Antologia*, 1899, vol. 84, pp. 576–85.

Parker, H., "A Possible Prime Minister," *Munsey's Magazine*, 1902, vol. 27, p. 224.

Peel, G., "The New Sir Robert Peel," *National Review*, 1903, vol. 41, p. 915.

Pemberton, T. E., "Early Career of Joseph Chamberlain," *Munsey's Magazine*, 1905, vol. 33, p. 32.

"Perennial Youth in English Politics," *Current Literature*, 1906, vol. 41, pp. 155–58.

Pigou, A. C., "The Known and the Unknown," *Fortnightly Review*, 1903, vol. 81, p. 36.

"Policy of Imperial Preference," *Littell's Living Age*, Dec. 12, 1903, vol. 239, pp. 641–55.

"Politics of Chamberlain," *Outlook*, 1903, vol. 74, pp. 921–22.

"Position of Chamberlain in 1886," *Spectator*, 1886, vol. 59, p. 1009.

"Protagonist and the Future," *Fortnightly Review*, 1903, vol. 80, pp. 734–46.

Roberts, C., "England's Colonial Secretary," *Everybody's Magazine*, 1902, vol. 8, p. 241.

Rose, J. C., "Hold on the Midlands," *Nation*, 1903, vol. 78, p. 163.

Russell, G. W. E., "Joseph Chamberlain, A Phase," *Cornhill Magazine*, 1914, n.s., vol. 37, pp. 310–17.

Salmon, E., "Imperial Policy," *Fortnightly Review*, 1903, vol. 79, pp. 638–45.

Salmon, E., "Mr. Chamberlain," *Fortnightly Review*, 1914, vol. 95, pp. 217–24.

Salmon, E., "New Chapter of Chamberlain," *Fortnightly Review*, 1902, vol. 79, p. 638.

Salmon, E., "Political Career," *Fortnightly Review*, 1914, vol. 101, pp. 217–24.

Seaman, O., "To the Memory of Joseph Chamberlain," *Littell's Living Age*, Aug. 8, 1914, vol. 282, pp. 375–76.

Sevin-Desplaces, L., "Chamberlain, Cecil Rhodes and Co.," *Revue Politique et Littéraire*, 1900, ser. 4, vol. 13, pp. 50–51.

Skottowe, B. C., "Joseph Chamberlain," *National Review*, 1896, vol. 27, p. 771.

Smith, G., "Chamberlain's Policy," *Independent*, June 18, 1903, vol. 55, pp. 1434–36.

Spender, H., "Sir William Peel and Joseph Chamberlain," *Fortnightly Review*, 1903, vol. 80, p. 598.

Stead, W. T., "Some Reputations in the Crucible of 1896," *Review of Reviews*, 1897, vol. 15, p. 56.

Stevens, F. G., "Chamberlain's Parallels," *Westminster Review*, 1906, vol. 165, pp. 1–9.

Story, D., "Biographical Sketch," *Munsey's Magazine*, 1901, vol. 26, pp. 396–401.

"Success of Joseph Chamberlain," *Saturday Review*, 1902, vol. 93, p. 197.

"Tariff Speech at Leeds," *Gunton's Magazine*, 1904, vol. 26, pp. 109–17.

Taylor, B., "Tariff Proposals of Chamberlain," *Nineteenth Century*, 1903, vol. 54, p. 839.

Thierry, C. de, "Chamberlain in the Colonial Office," *Contemporary Review*, 1900, vol. 78, pp. 365–80.

Thompson, R. E., "American View of the Proposals of Chamberlain," *Fortnightly Review*, 1903, vol. 80, p. 466.

"A Tribute to Chamberlain," *National Review*, 1902, vol. 39, p. 39.

Viallate, A., "Mr. Joseph Chamberlain," *Annales des Sciences Politique*, 1899, vol. 14, pp. 115–44.

Walters, G., "Cromwell and Chamberlain," *Arena*, 1900, vol. 24, p. 113.

Ward, Wilfred, "A Political Fabius Maximus," *Eclectic Magazine*, 1905, vol. 145, p. 382.

Whates, H., "Mr. Chamberlain," *Fortnightly Review*, 1900, vol. 74 (n.s., vol. 68), pp. 740–52.

White, F. A., "Chamberlain and Rosebery," *Westminster Review*, 1902, vol. 157, p. 385.

White, H., "Joseph Chamberlain," *Nation*, 1883, vol. 37, p. 48.

White, H., "Reactionary Protectionism of Chamberlain," *Nation*, 1902, vol. 76, p. 429.

Whiting, F. J., "Chamberlain vs. Chamberlain," *Nation*, 1903, vol. 78, pp. 124–25.

Wilson, R. F., "Joseph Chamberlain as I Knew Him," *United Empire*, 1915, n.s., vol. 8, pp. 102–11.

Wolf, L., "Tariff Proposals of Chamberlain," *World Today*, 1903, vol. 5, p. 1415.

Woods, Maurice, "Mr. Chamberlain," *Fortnightly Review*, 1914, vol. 96, pp. 197–211.